TARGETING

Air Force Doctrine Document 3-60
8 June 2006

Incorporating Change 1, 28 July 2011

This document complements related discussion found in Joint Publication 3-60, *Joint Targeting.*

Cover Sheet for Air Force Doctrine Document (AFDD) 3-60, *Targeting*

OPR: LeMay Center/DD

28 July 2011

AFDD numbering has changed to correspond with the joint doctrine publication numbering architecture (the AFDD titles remain unchanged until the doctrine is revised). Any AFDD citations within the documents will list the old AFDD numbers until the doctrine is revised. The changed numbers follow:

OLD	NEW	TITLE
AFDD 2-1	changed to AFDD 3-1	*Air Warfare*
AFDD 2-1.1	changed to AFDD 3-01	*Counterair Operations*
AFDD 2-1.2	changed to AFDD 3-70	*Strategic Attack*
AFDD 2-1.3	changed to AFDD 3-03	*Counterland Operations*
AFDD 2-1.4	changed to AFDD 3-04	*Countersea Operations*
AFDD 2-1.6	changed to AFDD 3-50	*Personnel Recovery Operations*
AFDD 2-1.7	changed to AFDD 3-52	*Airspace Control*
AFDD 2-1.8	changed to AFDD 3-40	*Counter-CBRN*
AFDD 2-1.9	changed to AFDD 3-60	*Targeting*
AFDD 2-10	changed to AFDD 3-27	*Homeland Operations*
AFDD 2-12	changed to AFDD 3-72	*Nuclear Operations*
AFDD 2-2	changed to AFDD 3-14	*Space Operations*
AFDD 2-2.1	changed to AFDD 3-14.1	*Counterspace Operations*
AFDD 2-3	changed to AFDD 3-24	*Irregular Warfare*
AFDD 2-3.1	changed to AFDD 3-22	*Foreign Internal Defense*
AFDD 2-4	changed to AFDD 4-0	*Combat Support*
AFDD 2-4.1	changed to AFDD 3-10	*Force Protection*
AFDD 2-4.2	changed to AFDD 4-02	*Health Services*
AFDD 2-4.4	changed to AFDD 4-11	*Bases, Infrastructure, and Facilities* [Rescinded]
AFDD 2-4.5	changed to AFDD 1-04	*Legal Support*
AFDD 2-5	changed to AFDD 3-13	*Information Operations*
AFDD 2-5.1	changed to AFDD 3-13.1	*Electronic Warfare*
AFDD 2-5.3	changed to AFDD 3-61	*Public Affairs Operations*
AFDD 2-6	changed to AFDD 3-17	*Air Mobility Operations*
AFDD 2-7	changed to AFDD 3-05	*Special Operations*
AFDD 2-8	changed to AFDD 6-0	*Command and Control*
AFDD 2-9	changed to AFDD 2-0	*ISR Operations*
AFDD 2-9.1	changed to AFDD 3-59	*Weather Operations*

BY ORDER OF THE
SECRETARY OF THE AIR FORCE

AIR FORCE DOCTRINE DOCUMENT 3-60
8 JUNE 2006
INCORPORATING CHANGE 1, 28 JULY 2011 |

SUMMARY OF CHANGES

This Interim change to Air Force Doctrine Document (AFDD) 2-1.9 changes the cover to AFDD 3-60, *Targeting* to reflect revised AFI 10-1301, Air Force Doctrine (9 August 2010). AFDD numbering has changed to correspond with the joint doctrine publication numbering architecture. AFDD titles and content remain unchanged until updated in the next full revision. A margin bar indicates newly revised material.

OPR: LeMay Center/DD
Certified by: LeMay Center/DD (Col Todd C. Westhauser)
Pages: 129
Accessibility: Available on the e-publishing website at www.e-publishing.af.mil for
        downloading
Releasability: There are no releasability restrictions on this publication
Approved by: LeMay Center/CC, Maj Gen Thomas K. Andersen, USAF
        Commander, LeMay Center for Doctrine Development and Education

FOREWORD

Time and time again in the last several decades, air and space power has proven among the most powerful of weapons in the nation's military arsenal, deciding some conflicts outright and enabling us to resolve others in the manner of our choosing. Today, air and space power can impose decisive effects anywhere on the globe at almost any time, but it has taken more than this global reach to make it the world's premier military instrument. Sound doctrine, strategy, and operational art are also required and the discipline of targeting is a vital piece of Air Force operational art.

Guided by sound doctrine and strategy, targeting during conflict enables air and space power to be a decisive force in modern warfare. Targeting processes and principles that encompass the realms of information and influence can also have decisive effects upon operations other than major combat. This publication describes what targeting is and how it supports the overarching structure of air and space planning, execution, and assessment. The United States military operates according to effects-based principles, which tie planning, execution, and assessment together into an adaptive whole. Accordingly, this publication also shows why and how effects-based thinking is integral to effective targeting today. This document builds upon the foundational doctrine concepts of an effects-based approach established in Air Force Doctrine Document 2, *Operations and Organization*.

Targeting has been a vital part of air and space power since the first weapon was dropped from an aircraft. It has evolved over a century from a matter of primitive guesswork into a discipline based on scientific principles and robust processes that is used to guide employment of much more than just weapons dropped from airplanes. Targeting will continue to evolve as it assimilates the insights of effects-based operations, improvements in battlespace awareness, and other innovations, but it will always be central to the way the Air Force conducts operations.

JAMES F. JACKSON
Brigadier General, USAF
Commander, Headquarters
Air Force Doctrine Center

TABLE OF CONTENTS

INTRODUCTION

PURPOSE

This Air Force Doctrine Document (AFDD) establishes doctrinal guidance for planning, executing, and assessing targeting operations.

APPLICATION

This AFDD applies to the Total Force: all Air Force military and civilian personnel, including regular, Air Force Reserve Command, and Air National Guard units and members.

Unless specifically stated otherwise, Air Force doctrine applies to the full range of military operations, as appropriate, from stability, security, transition, and reconstruction operations to major operations and campaigns.

The doctrine in this document is authoritative, but not directive. Therefore, commanders need to consider the contents of this AFDD and the particular situation when accomplishing their missions. Airmen should read it, discuss it, and practice it.

SCOPE

Air Force assets (people, weapons, and support systems) can be used across the range of military operations at the strategic, operational, and tactical levels of war. This AFDD discusses the fundamentals of organization and employment of Air Force air and space capabilities to accomplish the missions assigned by unified combatant commanders. More specific guidance on Air Force operations may be found in subordinate operational- and tactical-level doctrine documents.

COMAFFOR / JFACC / CFACC
A note on terminology

One of the cornerstones of Air Force doctrine is "the US Air Force prefers—and in fact, plans and trains—to employ through a commander, Air Force forces (COMAFFOR) who is also dual-hatted as a joint force air and space component commander (JFACC)." (AFDD 1)

To simplify the use of nomenclature, Air Force doctrine documents will assume the COMAFFOR is dual-hatted as the JFACC unless specifically stated otherwise. The term "COMAFFOR" refers to the Air Force Service component commander while the term "JFACC" refers to the joint operational commander.

While both joint and Air Force doctrine state that one individual will normally be dual-hatted as COMAFFOR and JFACC, the two responsibilities are different, and should be executed through different staffs.

Normally, the COMAFFOR function executes operational control/administrative control of Air Force forces through a Service A-Staff while the JFACC function executes tactical control of all joint air and space component forces through an air and space operations center.

When multinational operations are involved the JFACC becomes a combined forces air and space component commander (CFACC). Likewise, the air and space operations center (AOC), though commonly referred to simply as an AOC, in joint or combined operations is correctly known as a joint air and space operations center (JAOC) or combined air and space operations center (CAOC). Since nearly every operation the US conducts will involve international partners, this publication uses the terms CFACC and CAOC throughout to emphasize the doctrine's applicability to multinational operations.

FOUNDATIONAL DOCTRINE STATEMENTS

These statements are the basic principles and beliefs upon which this Air Force doctrine document (AFDD) is built. Other information in the AFDD expands on or supports these statements.

✪ Targeting is the process for selecting and prioritizing targets and matching appropriate actions to those targets to create specific desired effects that achieve objectives, taking account of operational requirements and capabilities. (Page 1)

✪ Targets are areas, complexes, installations, forces, equipment, capabilities, functions, individuals, groups, systems, or behaviors identified for possible action to support the commander's objectives, guidance, and intent. (Page 1)

✪ Targeting is a central component of Air Force operational art, forming an essential link between strategy and the tactical application of air and space power. (Page 1)

✪ Targeting helps translate strategy into discrete actions against targets by matching ways to means. (Page 1)

✪ Targeting is a command function and is inherently joint. It requires commander oversight and involvement to ensure proper execution. It is not the exclusive province of one division or type of personnel, but blends the expertise of many disciplines across the joint force. (Page 2)

✪ Targeting is integral to the air and space component's wartime battle rhythm and should always be thought of as part of a larger effects-based construct of planning, execution, and assessment. (Page 2)

✪ Targeting consists of two broad sets of responsibilities: those tied to a particular conflict and those that are ongoing, performed both in peace and war. (Page 2)

✪ Targeting is fundamentally effects-based. It is thus about more than just selecting targets for physical destruction. (Page 11)

✪ Targeting is integrated with other processes that create the overall campaign strategy and the joint air and space operations plan, the ongoing daily tasking cycle, and assessment that measures progress toward campaign objectives. (Page 11)

✪ Targeting is inherently estimative and anticipatory. Matching actions and effects to targets requires estimation and anticipation—prediction, in one sense—of future outcomes. (Page 12)

✪ Targeting is systematic. In supporting the commander's objectives, the tasking and targeting process seeks to achieve effects in a systematic manner. (Page 12)

✪ Assessment encompasses all efforts to evaluate effects and gauge progress toward accomplishment of effects and objectives. It also helps evaluate requirements for future action. (Page 57)

✪ To be useful as a gauge of effectiveness, a measure must be meaningful, reliable, and either observable or capable of being reliably inferred. (Page 58)

○ Regardless of the level of assessment, the process of analyzing the adversary, choosing appropriate measures, evaluating progress, and recommending action consists of the same four basic steps: Define, monitor, analyze, and recommend. (Page 66)

○ Targeting must adhere to the Law of Armed Conflict and must comply with all applicable rules of engagement. (Page 88)

CHAPTER ONE

TARGETING FUNDAMENTALS

Mere tonnage of explosives is a fallacious criterion. In the final analysis, victories are achieved because of the effect produced, not simply because of the effort expended.

—Brigadier General Haywood S. "Possum" Hansell, Jr., Memorandum to Army Air Force Chief of Staff General "Hap" Arnold, 26 July 1944

INTRODUCTION

Targeting is the process for selecting and prioritizing targets and matching appropriate actions to those targets to create specific desired effects that achieve objectives, taking account of operational requirements and capabilities.

Targeting applies to **targets**, which **are areas, complexes, installations, forces, equipment, capabilities, functions, individuals, groups, systems, or behaviors identified for possible action to support the commander's objectives, guidance, and intent**.

Targeting is a central component of Air Force operational art, forming an essential link between strategy and the tactical application of air and space power. Strategy allows planners and commanders to choose the best ways to attain desired outcomes. It melds ends (objectives and end states), ways (actions and effects of actions leading to the ends), means (resources needed and available to carry out planned actions), and risk (the probable "cost" of attaining the ends in terms of lives, equipment, effort, time, and opportunities). Strategy forms these into plans and guidance that can be used to task specific air and space assets through the tasking process and targeting. **Targeting helps translate strategy into discrete actions against targets by matching ways to means**. *Targeting also explicitly includes force execution and assessment, so it encompasses the processes and procedures that form the core of how the Air Force and the combined force as a whole fight at the operational level.*

The procedures and processes that comprise targeting form the core of how the Air Force and the joint force as a whole fights at the operational-level of war. Targeting, however, is but one component of an overarching approach to warfare and other operations that emphasizes achieving US objectives by imposing discrete, desired effects within the operational environment (OE). Within an effects-based framework, targeting helps determine the most effective and efficient means of creating desired effects. Outside of an effects-based framework, targeting can quickly devolve into simple attrition with availability of resources, not objectives and the end state, driving operations. Recent conflicts have shown that victory can be achieved more effectively and efficiently through an effects-based approach that extends beyond just attrition. Although there may be occasions when attrition is a desired effect that supports an objective, it is more often the result of planning without regard to the effects.

Targeting is a command function and is inherently joint. It requires commander oversight and involvement to ensure proper execution. It is not the exclusive province of one type of specialty or division, such as intelligence or operations, **but blends the expertise of many disciplines across the joint force.** Targeting occurs at every level of conflict, from strategic to tactical, and it is not solely the domain of airpower, but integrates the full spectrum of joint military capabilities to achieve the commander's objectives.

Targeting is an iterative and cyclic process. The "targeting cycle" is simply the discipline and process of selecting and prioritizing targets and matching actions to them. **Targeting is integral to the air and space component's wartime battle rhythm and should always be thought of as part of a larger effects-based construct of planning, execution, and assessment.**

Targeting is anticipatory and estimative in nature. In order to discriminately choose certain targets over others, targeteers (a term used throughout this publication to refer to specialists trained in analyzing targets and developing targeting solutions to support the commander's objectives) and other planners are anticipating and estimating that actions against those targets will be more effective and/or efficient than actions against other targets. Targeting seeks to exploit synergy between intelligence preparation of the battlespace (IPB); target development; intelligence, surveillance, and reconnaissance (ISR); strategy and planning; ISR employment; and assessment. An emerging Air Force concept currently labeled "predictive battlespace awareness" (PBA) attempts to capture that synergy. PBA is the situational awareness needed to develop patterns of behavior, constraints and opportunities of geography, topography, cultures, environment, and forces that allow us to misdirect, predict, and pre-empt our adversaries to successfully create effects when and where we choose. This concept requires an extremely high-fidelity model of the threat to provide a heretofore-unknown situational awareness capability to support effective targeting.

Saying that targeting is estimative and anticipatory—"predictive," in a very limited sense—does not imply that there is some magical formula, technique, or tool that will allow perfect anticipation of events, consequences, and reactions. The conduct of war and other military operations will always be a matter of art, and while tools and techniques can help make their planning, execution, assessment, and adaptation more effective and efficient, nothing can remove the elements of "friction" and uncertainty—nothing can replace the "art" in the "art of war."

Targeting consists of two broad sets of responsibilities: those tied to a particular conflict and those that are ongoing, performed both in peace and war.

The former are discussed in this document within an effects-based framework, covered in separate chapters on planning, execution, and assessment. A final chapter describes the continuous activities involved in targeting readiness and the responsibilities associated with support to warfighters that are not tied to particular conflicts or operations. These include such things as peacetime target development, creation and maintenance of targeting support architectures, influencing the development of munitions, and the training and equipping of targeting staffs. The three basic aspects of effects-based operations (EBO)—planning, employment, and assessment—cannot be divorced from one another.

When we discuss a "target," we speak of what the target itself brings to the fight—its intrinsic or acquired characteristics. When we wish to discuss how *we* regard the target—the things we attribute to it, the value or degree of sensitivity we place upon it, and the approach we take toward it, we are speaking of "targeting," the process used to define how we will act against the target.

The purpose of targeting and its associated processes is to provide commanders with a means of linking the end state to objectives designed to attain it, linking those objectives to subordinate effects at all levels, and linking the effects to specific actions against targets throughout the battlespace. The processes of planning, tasking, targeting, and assessing effects provide a logical progression that forms the basis of decision-making and ensures consistency with the commander's objectives and the end state.

The planning, tasking, and targeting processes are flexible enough to provide solutions in situations ranging from limited-scope, quick-reaction tactical operations to broad multiple-theater campaigns. In all situations, this primary focus is to assist the commander to most effectively employ air, space, and information resources to achieve joint force and national objectives.

TARGET CHARACTERISTICS

Every target has distinct intrinsic or acquired characteristics, the most important of which affect how the entity or behavior is targeted. Intrinsic characteristics are the initial, original, or designed characteristics a target. Acquired characteristics are changes that modify, enhance, or augment the intrinsic characteristics of the target. These characteristics form the basis for target detection, location, identification, and classification for future surveillance, analysis, strike, and assessment. In general, there are four categories of characteristics by which targets can be defined: *physical, environmental, functional,* and *cognitive.* These are briefly described below. The lists of example characteristics are not intended to be exhaustive, and some characteristics may belong in more than one category.

Physical Characteristics. These are features that describe what a target *is*. These are discernable to the five senses or through sensor-derived signatures. These may greatly affect the type and number of weapons, the weapon systems, and the methods or tactics employed against the target.

- ✪ Location.
- ✪ Shape.
- ✪ Size or area covered.
- ✪ Appearance (outward form and features, including color).
- ✪ Number and nature of elements.
- ✪ Dispersion or concentration of elements.
- ✪ Reflectivity (to heat, light, sound, radar energy, etc).
- ✪ Structural composition.
- ✪ Degree of hardening.
- ✪ Electromagnetic radiation (e.g., radar and radio transmissions).

Environmental Characteristics. These are features that describe the effect of the environment on the target and its surroundings. These characteristics may also affect the types and numbers of weapons, weapon systems, and the methods used to attack them.

- ✪ Atmospheric conditions affecting the target (temperature, visibility, etc).
- ✪ Terrain features (land form, vegetation, soil, elevation, etc).
- ✪ Degree of concealment, camouflage, and countermeasures.
- ✪ Physical relationships (such as proximity to noncombatants or friendly forces, etc.).
- ✪ Dependencies (raw materials, personnel, energy, water, command/control, etc.).

Functional Characteristics. These are features that describe what the target *does* and how it does it. They describe the target's function within the enemy system, how the target or system operates, its level of activity, the status of its functionality, and, in some cases, its importance to the enemy. Functional characteristics are often hard to discern, because they most often cannot be directly observed. Reaching plausible conclusions can often entail speculation and much deductive and inductive reasoning.

- ✪ Target's normal or reported activity.
- ✪ Target status (state or condition at a given point in time [e.g., "operational," "inoperative"]).
- ✪ Degree, proportion, or percentage of functionality (e.g., "function 50% degraded").
- ✪ Materials the target requires in order to perform its function(s).

✪ Functional redundancy (can the target's function be performed elsewhere or by something else?).

✪ Target's ability to reconstitute itself or its function.

✪ Target's mobility characteristics.

　✪✪ Fixed (unable to move).

　✪✪ Transportable (operate from fixed locations, but can be broken down and moved).

　✪✪ Mobile (operate on the move or with very limited setup time).

✪ Target's ability to defend itself.

✪ Target's role as an element of the enemy's system.

　✪✪ Target's importance within the enemy's strategic structure (such as its role in the geopolitical system or its cultural importance).

✪ If the target is a person or group, what other people or groups are necessary to enable him/her/it to function?

　✪✪ What is the nature of the connectivity between this person/group and others?

Cognitive Characteristics. Features that describe how some targets *think*, exercise control functions, or otherwise process information. These can be critical to how something is targeted and can be especially important from an effects-based perspective, where nonlethal, nonkinetic, or informational means of imposing effects are considered. These characteristics can also be critical to targeting an enemy system, since nearly every system possesses some central controlling function, and neutralizing this may be crucial to obtaining the desired behavior. As with functional characteristics, these are often difficult to discern or deduce.

✪ How the target processes information.

✪ How the target's decision cycle works (if applicable).

✪ Process inputs the target requires to perform its function(s).

✪ Outputs to the processes the target performs.

✪ How much information the target can handle.

✪ How the target or system stores information.

✪ If the target is a person or group of people.

　✪✪ How does the target think?

　✪✪ What are its motivations?

　✪✪ What behavior does the target exhibit?

THE TARGETING PROCESS

Viewed generically, outside the context of overarching processes and the battle rhythm, the targeting process consists of the following general phases, most of which dovetail into the planning and tasking processes once battle rhythm is established, but which also include activities that start before the battle rhythm and others that are accomplished apart from any operation or process within a specific contingency. This process is also used to guide targeting efforts that take place entirely outside the context of the air estimate and tasking processes. The basic targeting process consists of 6 stages, or "phases" (See Figure 1.1).

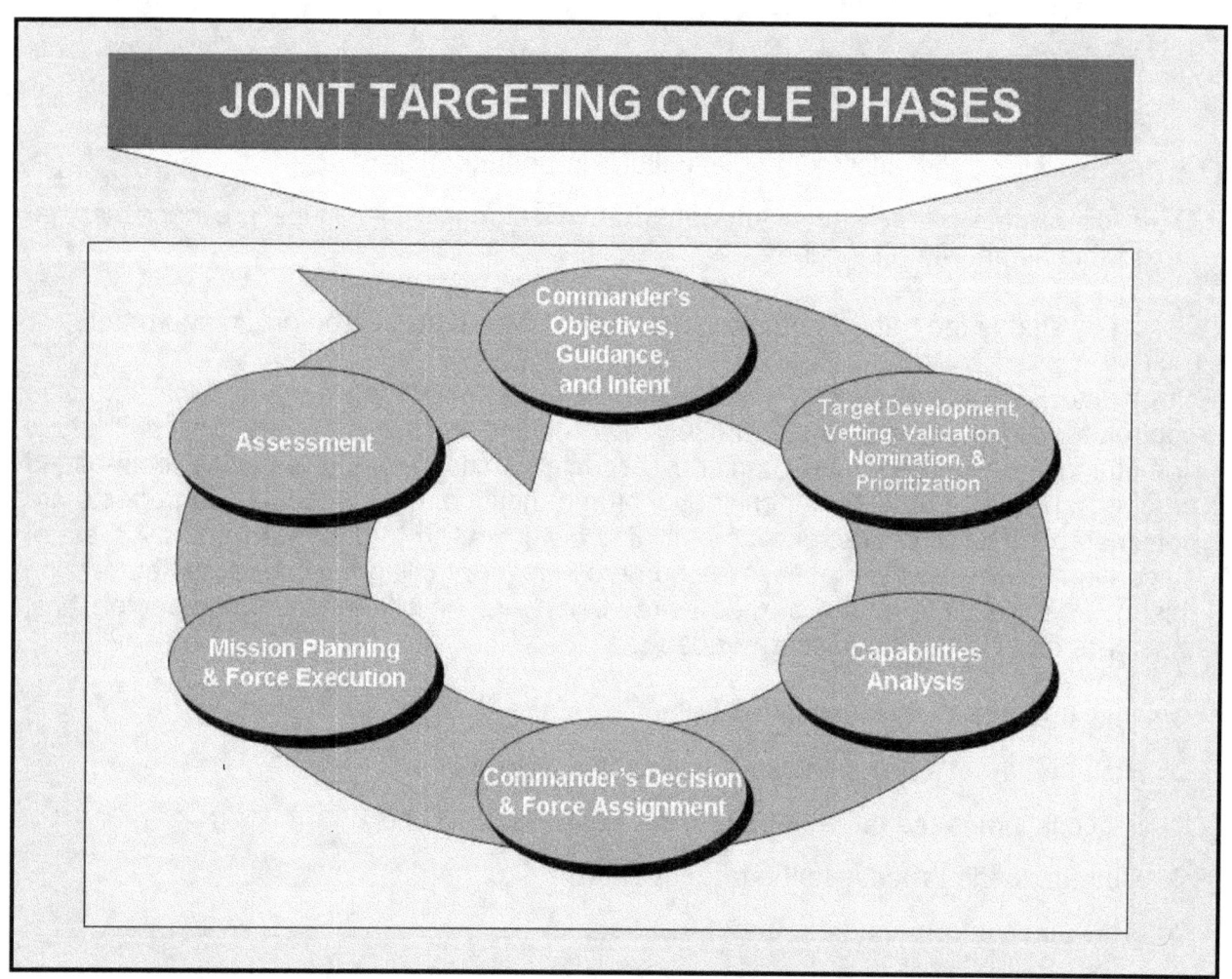

Figure 1.1. Joint Targeting Process Phases

✪ Commander's objectives, guidance and intent.

✪ Target development, vetting, validation, nomination, and prioritization.

- ✪ Capabilities analysis.
- ✪ Commander's decision and force assignment.
- ✪ Mission planning and force execution.
- ✪ Assessment.

Commander's objectives, guidance, and intent. This is the most important step in the joint targeting process, because it encapsulates all the national-level guidance in a set of outcomes relevant to the present situation and set the course for all that follows, even though these are determined during strategy development and not as part of the targeting process, per se. Many times, however, targeteers working before formal planning for a contingency begins or during normal peacetime operations may have to infer or make assumptions concerning these. This should be done using the best guidance available at the time. A good specific objective must be understandable, require action, be attainable, allow some room to reach the solution, and provide criteria for use in measuring both progress and effectiveness

Target development, vetting, validation, nomination, and prioritization. Target development is the systematic examination of potential target systems to determine the type and duration of action that must be exerted on each target to create desired effects that achieve the commander's objectives. Target vetting leverages the expertise of the national intelligence community to verify the fidelity of the intelligence and analysis used to develop the target(s). Target validation determines whether a target remains a viable element of a target system and whether it complies with the law of armed conflict (LOAC) and the rules of engagement. Once targets are developed, vetted, and validated, they are nominated for approval and action in a given time period. As part of this process, they are prioritized relative to all joint targets in a joint integrated prioritized target list (JIPTL), which is submitted to the combined force commander (CFC) for approval.

Capabilities analysis. This portion of the joint targeting process involves evaluating available capabilities against desired effects to determine the appropriate options available to the commander. The outputs of this stage inform the commander's estimate within the joint planning and execution system.

Commander's decision and force assignment. Once the CFC has approved the JIPTL, joint force components prepare tasking orders and release them to executing forces and units. The joint targeting process facilitates creation of tasking orders by providing amplifying information needed for detailed unit-level planning.

Mission planning and force execution. Upon receipt of tasking orders, tasked units perform detailed execution planning and perform their missions.

Assessment. All assessments related to targeting should be included here. This phase evaluates the effectiveness of operations and feeds development of future strategy, guidance, and adaptation to the adversary's actions.

Examining these stages in light of the air tasking cycle and its relationship to deliberate targeting, described in Chapter Two, it is easy to see that targeting is absolutely integral to the tasking process. Further detail concerning the joint targeting process can be found in Joint Publication (JP) 3-60, *Joint Targeting.*

TYPES OF TARGETING

There are two basic types of targeting: deliberate and dynamic.

Deliberate targeting is the procedure for prosecuting targets that are detected, identified, and developed in sufficient time to schedule actions against them in tasking cycle products such as the air and space tasking order (ATO). Targets prosecuted as part of deliberate targeting are known to exist in an operating area and have missions or actions scheduled against them, or have concepts of operations (CONOPS) developed to prosecute them with pre-planned on-call missions. Examples may range from targets on joint target lists in the joint air and space operations plan (JAOP) to new targets developed in sufficient time to list in an ATO. The deliberate targeting procedure is an integral part of the air tasking cycle, although aspects of it take place outside the tasking process per se. Deliberate targeting is discussed further in Chapter Two.

Dynamic targeting is the procedure for prosecuting targets that are not detected, identified, or developed in time to be included in deliberate targeting, and therefore have not had actions scheduled against them. Targets prosecuted as part of dynamic targeting are previously unanticipated, unplanned, or newly detected and are generally of such importance to a component, the CFC, or higher authority that they warrant prosecution within the current execution period. If the target is not critical or time-sensitive enough to warrant prosecution during the current execution period, the target may be developed for prosecution during a later execution period. Analysis of the target may also determine that no action is needed. Dynamic targeting is covered further in Chapter Three.

Target "Sensitivity." Certain targets require special care or caution in treatment because failure to target them or to target them properly can lead to major adverse consequences. Examples might include leadership targets that must be handled sensitively due to potential political repercussions, targets located in areas with a high risk of collateral civilian damage, or weapons of mass destruction (WMD) facilities, where improper targeting can lead to major long-term environmental damage. Such targets are often characterized as "sensitive" in one respect or another, but calling them "sensitive targets" is incorrect, since the "sensitivity" is attributed to them by us and is not an intrinsic characteristic. Nonetheless, the manner in which they are *targeted* is sensitive and may require coordination with and approval from the CFC or higher authorities. In most cases, it is best to establish criteria for engaging such targets in as much detail as possible during planning, before combat commences. These considerations are covered further in Chapter Two.

"Time-sensitivity" is a somewhat different matter. Many targets may be fleeting; many may be critical to operations. Those that are both present one of the biggest targeting challenges faced by the joint force. Advances in surveillance technology and weaponry make it possible in some instances to detect, track, and engage high-priority targets in real time, or to thwart emerging enemy actions before they become dangerous to the joint force. Joint doctrine calls the targets prosecuted in this manner "time-sensitive targets" (TST): "those targets requiring immediate response because they pose (or will soon pose) a danger to friendly forces or are highly lucrative, fleeting targets of opportunity." (JP 1-02) The CFC provides specific guidance and priorities for TSTs within the operational area. Examples might be things like a weapons of mass destruction (WMD)-capable combat vessel that was just detected approaching the joint force, a sought-after enemy national leader whose location was just identified; an enemy aircraft detected approaching friendly high-value assets, or an intermediate-range ballistic missile launch. The CFC designates TSTs. However, there may be other targets requiring "time-sensitive" treatment, which are of concern primarily to the CFC's component commanders (vital to their schemes of maneuver or immediately threatening their forces, for instance) that the CFC may not deem to be TSTs. These targets are prosecuted using the same dynamic targeting methodology as TSTs, even though they may not be designated as such and even though their prosecution may be tasked and tracked by different elements in the combined air and space operations center (CAOC). TST prosecution is a special form of dynamic targeting and is covered further in Chapter Three.

Targeting is the shared responsibility of operations personnel, planners, and intelligence analysts at all levels of command within a joint force. Targeting and attack functions are accomplished in accordance with the LOAC and international agreements and conventions, as well as rules of engagement (ROE) approved by the President and Secretary of Defense for a particular operation. Military commanders, planners, and legal experts must consider the desired end state and political aims when making targeting decisions. These issues are dealt with further in Appendix A.

TARGETING AND TARGETING-RELATED RESPONSIBILITIES

The combined forces air and space component commander (CFACC) has the following targeting responsibilities:

☢ Plan, coordinate, integrate, task, and direct the joint air and space effort in accordance with the CFC's guidance and joint force objectives.

☢ Develop a JAOP derived from the CFC's broader objectives for the operation, and guidance regarding the roles, missions, tasks, and responsibilities of joint air and space capabilities and forces. This responsibility is further elaborated in Chapter Two.

☢ After consulting with other component commanders, recommend apportionment of the joint air effort that should be devoted to various air operations for a given period of time (see Chapter Two).

○ Translate air apportionment into allocation and develop targeting guidance into the ATO, which may include specific aim points/desired points of impact (see Chapter Two).

○ Direct and ensure deconfliction of joint air operations (see Chapters Two and Three).

○ Integrate and synchronize joint air operations (see Chapter Two).

○ Coordinate with the appropriate components, national agencies, and liaison elements for synchronization and deconfliction with land and maritime operations (see Chapter Two).

○ Coordinate with the appropriate components' agencies and liaison elements for tasking of the capabilities and forces made available (see Chapter Two).

○ Monitor execution and redirect joint air and space operations as required (see Chapter Three).

○ Compile component target requirements and prioritize targets based on CFC guidance (see Chapters Two and Three).

○ Establish ROE and special instructions (SPINS) that clearly state combat identification (CID) requirements (for example, which CID systems will be used, who can declare a track "hostile," etc.) (see Chapters Two and Three).

○ Accomplish tactical and operational assessment and support accomplishment of campaign and national assessment (see Chapter Four).

Unit-level intelligence teams have the responsibility to support targeting in these key areas:

○ Verify the targeting guidance in the ATO, which often includes review of desired point of impact (DPI) coordinates against imagery and adjudication of suspected errors with the CAOC.

○ Ensure the integrity of targeting data provided to the mission planning process, which may include manual verification of coordinates, elevations, weapon azimuths, impact angles, and fuzing instructions whenever direct electronic transfer of such data is not possible.

○ Assisting in the performance of tactical assessment, through, for example, the timely dissemination of mission reports (MISREPS).

Units and personnel tasked with the execution of tactical actions against targets have the following responsibilities:

○ Comply with all ROE and SPINS applicable to targeting, especially with respect to CID responsibilities (see Chapter Three).

- Confirm CID of the target as hostile before taking action against it (see Chapter Three).

- Submitting timely MISREPs and otherwise supporting tactical assessment efforts.

PRINCIPLES OF TARGETING

Targeting is focused on achieving objectives. The purpose of strategy is to create a mechanism whereby the commander's objectives—and ultimately the end state—can be achieved. *Targeting is the embodiment of strategy where courses of action, objectives, and effects are developed into detailed actions against targets.* Like all other components of strategy, targeting must focus on attaining the objectives. Every target nominated should in some way contribute to attaining the commander's objectives and end state.

Targeting is fundamentally effects-based. It is about more than just the selection of targets for physical destruction. Some may regard targeting as only concerned with how to cause physical destruction, but this is a very limited—and limiting—perspective. Destruction may still be the best means to the end, but it is only one effect within a spectrum of possible options. Typically, it is a first step en route to other, higher-order indirect effects and objectives. The underlying premise of an effects-based approach is that it is possible to direct power (of all kinds) against targets in ways that cause military and political effects beyond the mere destruction of those targets—that ultimately cause desired changes in enemy behavior. Targeting should consider all possible means to achieve desired effects, drawing from all available forces, weapons, and platforms.

Targeting is integrated with other processes that create the overall campaign strategy and the JAOP, the ongoing daily tasking cycle that ultimately produces tasking orders, and assessment that measures progress toward campaign objectives. It cannot be separated from the overarching set of processes without turning it into an inputs-based exercise in target servicing—taking a target list determined by someone else, matching available resources to those targets, and waiting blindly for subsequent guidance, which usually devolves into simple attrition. Integrating targeting within these overarching processes enables an effects-based approach.

Targeting is *interdisciplinary, requiring the efforts of personnel from many functional disciplines.* For example, strategists and other planners bring knowledge of the larger context and overarching plans, operators bring experience gained from combat execution, while intelligence personnel provide analysis of enemy strengths and vulnerabilities. Judge advocates provide expertise in the application of the LOAC, as well as application and interpretation of ROE, while personnel with geospatial expertise provide data vital for mission planning and weapons delivery. An effects-based approach to targeting is fundamentally a team effort.

Targeting is inherently estimative and anticipatory. Matching actions and effects to targets requires estimating and anticipating future outcomes. In some cases the outcome is straightforward, such as anticipating that disabling a fire control radar will put a surface-to-air missile battery out of action. In most cases, however, estimation is more complicated. Many factors contribute to successful targeting. IPB should yield insight on the enemy and his intentions. Target system analysis yields understanding of how components of the enemy system interact and how the system functions as a whole. ISR assets gather needed data and help improve the accuracy and extent of estimation. Such analyses enable planners to select targets and methods of affecting them that increase the probability of desired outcomes and make the most efficient use of limited air and space resources. This does not imply perfect knowledge or anticipation; uncertainty and friction still apply.

Targeting is systematic. In supporting the commander's objectives, the targeting process seeks to achieve effects in a systematic manner. Targeting, like the other processes that it complements, is a rational, iterative process that methodically analyzes, prioritizes, and assigns forces against adversary targets to achieve the effects needed to meet campaign objectives. If the desired effects are not achieved, targets are "recycled" through the tasking process, or different targets are selected.

The principles set forth above establish a broad framework on which the targeting discipline should build. To put them in proper context, however, one must understand what targets are and how they are prosecuted, as well as what targeting responsibilities the commander of air and space forces has. The sections below describe targets, the two basic types of targeting, and commanders' responsibilities, all of which are explored further in the following chapters.

We are running an effects-based campaign that is partially kinetic, partially non-kinetic, partially information operations. And so what we judge effectiveness by is not just whether there is a hole in the room of a building, but whether or not the function that the element did before ceases to be effective.

—Maj Gen Stanley A. McChrystal
Vice Director of Operations, Joint Staff
Dept. of Defense news conference on Operation
IRAQI FREEDOM, 22 March 2003

EFFECTS-BASED APPROACH TO OPERATIONS

To understand how targeting forms one pillar of a flexible system that can accommodate many different strategies and achieve a wide variety of objectives through a wide variety of means, it is first necessary to understand the effects-based approach and how targeting fits within it.

In the most fundamental sense, an *effects-based approach is one in which operations are planned, executed, assessed, and adapted to influence or change systems or capabilities in order to achieve desired outcomes.* That is, they seek to understand and exploit the complex connections among individual actions, the effects—direct and indirect—that those actions produce, how those effects influence the states and behaviors of complex systems in the OE, and how these effects contribute to the accomplishment of ultimate desired outcomes. *An effect is the physical or behavioral state of a system that results from an action, a set of actions, or another effect* Effects and their accompanying causal linkages join actions to objectives. The actions and effects in any causal chain can derive from any element of national power—economic, political/diplomatic, military, or informational, and may occur at any point across the range of operations from peace to global conflict. Properly understanding the relationship among effects at all levels is important to planning and conducting any campaign.

Air Corps Tactical School faculty, late 1930s

At least as far back as World War II, some air planners were trying to implement the essential concepts of [an effects-based approach]. In the late 1930's, particularly at the Air Corps Tactical School, U.S. Army Air Corps (USAAC) thinkers had developed a number of theories about air warfare, including one which became known as the industrial-web theory. This theory was actually quite well grounded in concepts that became known as effects-based. The basic idea was that a modern war machine, such as the German or Japanese armies of the time, required the support of a huge industrial complex comprised of many interlinked sub elements called a web.

Manufacturing plants, transportation systems, power production, delivery systems, and other critical elements made up this web. Further, there were thought to be a finite number and determinable number of vital links of what we now call critical nodes, which if successfully destroyed or debilitated, would bring about collapse of the entire web. (Eventually, this theory was used to develop Air War Planning Document [AWPD]-1, the plan that guided expansion of the USAAC during the early 40's and initial strategy development for the Combined Bomber Offensive against the Germans prior to 1943.)

—Edward C. Mann, Gary Endersby, and Thomas R. Searle,
Thinking Effects: Effects-Based Methodology for Joint Operations

Some methods that we call effects-based today have always been part of well-waged war, but they have rarely been part of a systematic approach. Capabilities like precision engagement and rapid global mobility—the fruits of technological advance—have made possible a range of effects that were not possible before. Thus, commanders today have the capability to do such things as coerce changes in enemy behavior while minimizing unintended destruction, set operational tempos that adversaries cannot match, effectively anticipate enemy courses of action in some cases, and dominate enemy decision cycles. In past eras, commanders had to rely on their own intuition to apply effects-based methods. Today, the much greater range of possible effects, the sophistication of the capabilities used to impose them, and the increasing realization that costly force-on-force warfare is politically, economically, and even morally difficult, make a systematic approach to EBO necessary. The section below recapitulates the basic principles of an effects-based approach to military operations found in Air Force Doctrine Document (AFDD) 2, *Operations and Organization,* and ties those principles into the targeting discipline specifically. It is vital to remember, however, that *many effects are created through processes other than targeting. All instruments of national power should be considered in an effects-based approach, and even within the context of force-on-force engagement, such functions as air mobility and ISR can create effects that are crucial to achievement of objectives, or that can substitute for the offensive application of force* in some circumstances. This publication, however, focuses upon how effects can be achieved through targeting.

PRINCIPLES OF EBO

These principles are included here in abbreviated form for ease of reference (see AFDD 2):

- ✪ Planning, employment, and assessment should be inextricably linked and an effects-based approach should attempt to meld them as seamlessly as possible.

- ✪ EBO should focus on achievement of objectives and end state; all intended effects should logically support their achievement and objectives at all levels must be logically tied together; in this sense, EBO is an elaboration of "strategy-to-task."

- ✪ EBO are about creating effects, not about the platforms, weapons, or methods used to create them.

- ✪ EBO should consider all possible types of effects, not just destruction and attrition (although these can still be very viable elements of strategy).

- ✪ EBO should seek to achieve objectives most effectively, then most efficiently; accomplishing the mission comes first, but within that constraint accomplishment should be sought while minimizing cost in lives, treasure, time, and/or opportunities.

- ✪ EBO cut across all disciplines, dimensions, and echelons of conflict and operations; operations should integrate all appropriate instruments of power, all component efforts, and exploit the fact that tactical actions can have direct operational or strategic consequences.

- ✪ An effects-based approach recognizes that conflict is a clash of complex adaptive systems.

✪✪ Planning must always account for how the adversary will respond to planned actions.

✪✪ Warfare is complex and non-linear; many rules that apply in simple linear models and wargames don't apply in the real world.

✪✪ Cause and effect are often not easy to trace, especially for indirect effects.

✪ EBO focus upon behavior, not just in physical states or changes—this can include the behavior of friendly and neutral actors as well as that of the adversary.

✪ EBO recognize that comprehensive knowledge of all actors and of the operational environment are important to success, but come at a price.

✪ EBO should always consider the "law of unintended consequences;" "no plan survives first contact with the enemy" without adapting.

✪ EBO are a comprehensive way of thinking about conflict that must consider the full range of military operations, from peace to war and back to peace.

✪ EBO are not new; most of these principles have intuitively been part of well-waged war for millennia.

TARGETING CONSIDERATIONS FOR STABILITY OPERATIONS

Targeting is a discipline that is relevant across the entire range of military operations. This publication emphasizes the critical role targeting plays as part of the ongoing battle rhythm in major combat, because that relationship is highly complex. Nonetheless, the reader should realize that targeting and effects-based principles are at least as applicable during stability operations as during major combat. The following considerations distinguish stability operations in general and targeting during them in particular:

✪ There will be a greater emphasis on non-kinetic actions and peaceful uses of air and space power, such as air mobility and ISR. While these uses are vital to major combat operations, they may comprise the only uses of air and space power in some stability situations.

✪ There will be closer integration among the various components of the joint force and the air and space component may often be employed in support of tactical operations on the ground.

✪ There will be more thorough integration of all instruments of national power and a greater emphasis upon the political and economic consequences of action than in major combat operations.

✪ There may be a need to integrate targeting efforts with the efforts of non-Department of Defense (DOD) governmental agencies, such as the State Department, and nongovernmental organizations, such as the International Red

Cross, or with the governments of other nations. Such organizations may also hold veto power over targeting decisions made by military commanders.

- ✪ There may be more direct interest in and influence on operations from high-level leadership such as unified combatant commanders, the Secretary of Defense, and the President.

- ✪ There may be greater emphasis upon minimizing collateral damage (CD) and CD risk calculations may be scrutinized by higher-level leaders than in major combat operations. This concern for reduced CD usually results in stability operations having more restrictive ROE than typical major combat operations, and targeteers can expect a much larger restricted target list (RTL). All planners and operators must remain aware of greatly increased potential negative results of even a single misplaced weapon under these circumstances.

- ✪ In many stability operations, lack of large numbers of viable identified targets drives the bulk of force application into dynamic targeting, such as that executed through close air support (CAS) or on-call air interdiction missions. This fact, coupled with the need for minimization of CD, puts added stress on the entire dynamic targeting "kill chain." This requires airtight command and control for both the air and ground components, especially in situations where the bulk of force application occurs in small numbers of ground force troops-in-contact situations. Proper use of and coordination with elements such as the air support operations center (ASOC), the tactical air control party (TACP), and the battlefield coordination detachment (BCD), as well as clear and rapid communications into the CAOC operations division, are mandatory for success.

- ✪ Kinetic actions may have to be more thoroughly integrated with non-kinetic means and may entail targeting combat actions quite close to areas where operations such as peace enforcement and humanitarian assistance are being conducted.

- ✪ There may be a greater emphasis on timely tactical assessment of actions and upon thorough operational assessment on a shorter timeline than is customary in major combat operations. Interest in assessments may also come from higher leadership or non-military organizations.

CHAPTER TWO

DELIBERATE TARGETING

Strategy is the employment of battle to gain the end in war; it must therefore give an aim to the whole military action, which must be in accordance with the object of the war; in other words, strategy forms the plan of the war.

—Carl von Clausewitz

GENERAL

Planning encompasses all the means through which strategies and courses of action (COA) are developed, such as contingency and crisis action planning, as well as operational or campaign design. The latter encompasses the joint air and space estimate process (JAEP) that produces the JAOP. Since it sets the stage for all other actions, planning is where sound, effects-based principles have the largest play and may have the greatest impact on operations. Plans must tie objectives and effects at all levels, and actions together into a logical, coherent whole.

Targeting supports operational-level planning by helping validate that elements of a plan are feasible or are not cost-prohibitive in terms of resource expenditure, and by helping create the detailed tactical-level products for the opening phases of action that are usually appended to operational-level plans. The objectives, guidance, and intent derived during planning, however, guide all efforts, including targeting, throughout employment and assessment as well. This serves to tie planning, employment, and assessment together inextricably. Further, planning continues once operations commence and the battle rhythm is under way. Operational planning continues as enemy actions are evaluated or anticipated through revision of strategy and implementation of branches and sequels. All of the tactical-level action conducted during employment requires planning as well. In fact, the majority of physical planning effort supports tactical action once operations commence.

Targeting support to formal operational planning and the deliberate targeting that is conducted once operations begin are both accomplished through the deliberate targeting procedure described in this chapter. Again, *deliberate targeting is the procedure for prosecuting targets that are detected, identified, and developed in sufficient time to schedule actions against them in tasking cycle products such as the ATO.* Deliberate targeting handles targets in one of two ways: 1) plans and schedules specific actions against specific targets, and 2) creates on-call packages or missions that deal with targets through predetermined CONOPS. Preplanned missions are typically used against fixed targets or targets that are transportable, but operate in fixed locations. However, deliberate targeting can be used against mobile targets, especially when the target is in a defensive posture and may be in positions for long periods of time. On-call missions can be used against fixed, transportable, and mobile targets. For instance, a fixed building may be watched, but does not become a target until some critical person, group, or equipment arrives, at which time the on-call mission is scheduled on the tasking order if intelligence arrives in sufficient time. Other potential targets that are detected or become significant during the current execution period (once all formal products of the planning and tasking processes are issued), including the CFC's TSTs, are dealt with using dynamic targeting (see Chapter Three).

The effects-based principles set forth in AFDD 2 should guide all planning efforts, including deliberate targeting. The spectacular success US forces have enjoyed in major combat operations since Operation DESERT STORM was made possible in large part by their ability to exploit the full range of effects beyond simple destruction and attrition. This is an advantage that the effects-based approach confers. An effects-based approach is even more critical for success in stability operations such as counterinsurgency and peace enforcement, because they rely more on "non-kinetic" means and less on types of effects for which cause and effect are well understood, like attrition. To exploit the full range of possible effects in a given situation, planners must understand what effects are, how they relate to actions and objectives, and how various types of effects can be exploited to yield desired outcomes.

Two general targeting methodologies exist, each approaching the problem from opposite points of view. The first focuses on inputs to the battle; it concentrates mechanically on the number of sorties and ordnance delivered. The second approach is based upon outputs. In this technique, the selected targets flow from the commander's intent and desired objectives…. Given a desired system-wide failure, what components will provide the necessary failure when destroyed? The process is analogous to determining what will cause a bridge to collapse, for example, rather than asking about the effects of destroying a single supporting pier.

—Steven M. Rinaldi,
Beyond the Industrial Web:
Economic Synergies and Targeting Methodologies

EFFECTS-BASED CONSIDERATIONS FOR PLANNING

Details concerning the taxonomy of effects can be found in AFDD 2. For the sake of convenience, this section presents a short recapitulation of the basic concepts. In the most basic sense, effects-based planning takes account of actions against specific targets, which lead to certain effects, which in turn lead to achievement of objectives. *Targeting is integral to an effects-based approach, because it is how targets are analyzed to determine how to create desired effects and where specific actions against those targets are determined.* Targets and actions are tactical-level entities. Effects and causal linkages join actions against targets to objectives and the end state. Effects thus exist at all levels of conflict, from the tactical to the strategic.

Effects can be intended or unintended and direct or indirect. Intended and unintended are straightforward in meaning. A *direct effect is the first-order result of action with no intervening mechanism between act and outcome*—usually immediate and empirically verifiable, like the results of weapons employment. Indirect effects are more complicated. *An indirect effect is a second-, third-, or nth-order effect created through an intermediate effect or causal linkage following a tactical action*—usually a delayed and/or displaced consequence associated with the action that caused the direct effect(s). Objectives are achieved through an accumulation of direct and indirect effects, but the effects sought at the strategic and operational levels are almost invariably indirect.

Indirect effects are often categorized as physical, psychological, or behavioral; are assessed functionally or systemically; and can be imposed cumulatively or in a cascading manner, sequentially or in parallel. Physical effects materially alter a system or target and are most important at the tactical level. Psychological effects are those that impact reasoning, emotion, and motivation and result in behavioral effects— measurable changes in behavior. These are most important at the operational and strategic levels of conflict. Functional effects relate to how well a system performs its intended function(s) and systemic effects relate to how well that system functions as a component of larger systems. These are most important for assessment considerations. Effects can accumulate over time, leading to gradual change, or can cause cascading change that occurs catastrophically and ripples through related and subordinate systems. Often, there are both cumulative and cascading components to effects, as when an enemy unit "breaks" in combat due to accumulated physical and psychological damage, but fails catastrophically at some point, affecting other units around it. Generally, it is best to attempt to cause cascading change or failure when possible. Effects can also be imposed sequentially or in parallel. Effects imposed in series, one after another over time, are sequential. Those imposed near-simultaneously are parallel effects, which place greater stress upon targeted systems and require faster adaptation. Parallel effects are generally preferable to sequential effects when it is possible to impose them. Full understanding of the types of effects and the principles of effects-based thinking can offer commanders more options, hasten success, and lead to success at lower "cost" in terms of lives, treasure, time, and opportunities. For further discussion of effects, with examples of the types mentioned above, see AFDD 2, Chapter Five.

TARGETING RESPONSIBILITIES DURING FORMAL PLANNING

Targeteers and other planners should keep the foregoing effects-based concepts in mind while building formal plans and conducting ongoing deliberate targeting once operations begin. Targeting supports every form of employment planning for joint operations. Joint operations planning employs an integrated process for orderly and coordinated problem solving and decision-making. In its peacetime application, the process is highly structured to support the thorough and fully coordinated development of contingency plans. In crisis, the process is shortened as needed to support the dynamic requirements of changing events. In wartime, the process adapts to accommodate greater decentralization of joint operation planning activities. Joint operation planning is conducted through one of the three following processes.

⊙ **Contingency planning** is conducted principally in peacetime to develop joint operation plans for contingencies identified in strategic planning documents. It prepares for possible contingencies based on the best available information and uses forces and resources apportioned in strategic planning documents. It relies heavily on assumptions about political and military circumstances that will exist when the plan is implemented.

⊙ **Crisis action planning** (CAP) is based on current events and is conducted in time-sensitive situations and emergencies using assigned, attached, and allocated forces and resources (i.e., is based on actual circumstances vice assumptions). This planning is more flexible and responsive to changing events.

⊙ **Operational Design/Campaign Planning** translates national and theater strategy into strategic and operational concepts through development of plans for theater campaigns. They embody that commander's strategic vision for the arrangement of related operations necessary to attain theater strategic objectives. Portions of this process are often delegated to components, which create plans to support the

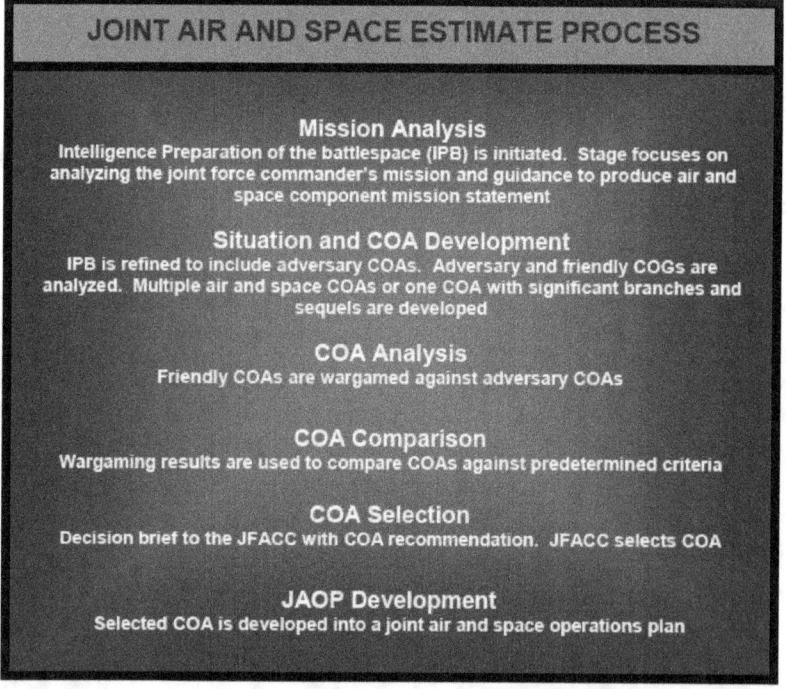

Figure 2.1. The Joint Air and Space Estimate Process

combatant commander's vision. *The air and space contribution to operational design/campaign planning is the JAOP.* This planning may take place independently or in support of deliberate planning and may continue through CAP.

The three processes are interrelated. All three may be conducted at different times for a given contingency and products created in one process are often used in others. For instance, a JAOP that is created as part of a theater CFACC's campaign planning done in support of deliberate planning efforts may be taken "off the shelf" and used in CAP as a particular contingency unfolds and may then be executed as the air and space campaign plan once the crisis becomes open conflict.

The JAOP is created through the JAEP. Almost all targeting support to pre-conflict planning is accomplished through the JAEP. Targeting support is vital during three of the six JAEP stages: mission analysis, situation and COA development, and JAOP development. See Figure 2.1.

Mission Analysis. During this stage, IPB is started. In order to fully support an effects-based campaign, the intelligence community must conduct robust IPB to use as the foundation for planning. IPB is the first "pillar" of PBA, which provides a comprehensive framework for ISR support to planning and COA selection. Consequently, IPB must assist commanders in anticipating enemy intent and enable them in pre-empting enemy actions.

The IPB process continues throughout planning by examining adversary and friendly capabilities, adversary intent, and the operational environment. Enemy and friendly centers of gravity (COG) are also identified during this initial stage of the JAEP. As mission analysis is refined through later stages of the JAEP, enemy COGs are analyzed, yielding critical vulnerabilities or other key system nodes. These are further examined through target system or nodal analysis to yield target sets, targets, critical elements, and aimpoints. Such analysis carries a considerable information-flow cost, however. In order to properly identify collection and exploitation requirements for targeting, *target system analysis must begin well in advance of operations and must continue throughout them.* It must begin during the initial stages of IPB and draw upon as much ongoing peacetime targeting material as is available for the theater or area of operations.

Situation and COA Development. IPB is refined during this stage and includes detailed analysis of COGs identified during mission analysis. COG analysis is important to targeting efforts because it identifies the enemy's sources of power and will to fight and tries to discover how and where those sources of power are vulnerable, where critical nodes within them are, and how they can be exploited. Two of the most common techniques for COG analysis usually yield insight on enemy systems that can be exploited to derive target sets and individual targets. The first is the "strategic ring" model, which divides the enemy "organism" into systems along functional lines (like leadership, organic essentials (resources), infrastructure, population, and defense or fighting mechanisms). This technique often yields useful target sets in each of the categories, but contains another important insight: leadership and control mechanisms (usually depicted as the central ring) are always a COG and almost always yield useful targets as analysis expands into target development. The two most common variations on this technique are the five-ring model (using the rings specified above) and similar seven-ring "national elements of value" model. Another common technique begins with the COG as a source of power, identifies the inherent abilities that allow it to act as such ("critical capabilities"), identifies the essential conditions, resources, or means ("critical requirements") that allow the critical capabilities to operate, and then determines where those critical requirements are vulnerable ("critical vulnerabilities"). While it can sometimes be difficult to pick critical vulnerabilities from critical requirements or translate the former into explicit target sets, target system and nodal analysis performed during target development can help "operationalize" this technique's insights.

JAOP Development. Operations are built from the top down, starting with the end state, leading to objectives at the highest levels, determining subordinate objectives needed to support those, then determining the effects needed to accomplish the objectives, and finally determining the actions necessary to create those effects. This stage and its ultimate product, the JAOP, describe how air and space forces will support the CFC's campaign plan. The JAOP identifies objectives, desired effects, targets, and assessment measures in as much detail as available time and intelligence allow. Objectives and the end state are products of commander's guidance, strategy development and planning, and while targeting efforts must always aim toward achieving them, they are not determined through the targeting process itself. Targeting is integral to JAOP development and deliberate targeting is used to help determine and develop target sets and targets included in the JAOP and its attachments (which may include full ATOs for the first day[s] of the conflict). Even if targeting information developed during planning is not included in the JAOP or its attachments, JAOP development requires considerable targeting effort in order to validate selected COAs, CONOPS, and other elements of the plan. Commanders and planners must know, at least approximately, how much effort and what resources are required to achieve the campaign's desired effects. The only way to learn this is to conduct some (at least notional) deliberate targeting well before the conflict begins. Target selection should be based upon desired effects against enemy COGs, which in turn should be based upon the objectives for the conflict.

The JAOP should be effects-based. It is the air and space component's main source of guidance for effects throughout the campaign and must make use of the principles and planning considerations set forth here. Targeting efforts play a major role in building an effects-based JAOP by relating effects to particular targets and helping validate whether planned resources can achieve those effects.

The JAOP should provide broad guidelines for prioritizing targets, making clear which categories or sets are most important to the campaign. The JAOP should also provide guidance on the sequencing of targeting actions or effects, which is not the same thing as priority. Although parallel effects are generally best, sometimes some targets must be attacked first to enable effects against other targets.

The JAOP, as well as subsequently published SPINS, air and space operations directives (AOD), and ATOs, must clearly articulate the commander's ROE that ensure operations comply with the LOAC. *The JAOP and subsequent planning guidance must also establish appropriate control and coordination measures.* Commanders may employ various maneuver and movement control, airspace control, and fire support coordination measures (FSCM) to facilitate effective joint operations. These measures include, but are not limited to, boundaries, phase lines, objectives, coordinating altitudes to deconflict air operations, air defense areas, amphibious objective areas, submarine operating patrol areas, and minefields.

Combat Identification. CID plays a critical role in all measures focused on the battlespace, such as dominant maneuver, precision engagement, full dimensional protection, and focused logistics, and has direct impact on the joint force's ability to support the CFC and to employ capabilities to maintain maximum effectiveness and minimize fratricide. CID is the capability to attain an accurate characterization of detected objects in the joint battlespace that enables high confidence and timely application of military options and weapons. Depending on the situation and the operational decisions that must be made, this characterization may be limited to "enemy," "friend," or "neutral." In other situations, other characterizations may be required—including, but not limited to, class, type, nationality, mission configuration, status, and intent. Planning guidance must clearly state CID requirements, including such things as which CID systems will be used, who will have authority to declare a track or potential target hostile, etc. For further guidance on CID, see JP 3-33, *Joint Task Force Headquarters,* and Air Force Tactics, Techniques, and Procedures (AFTTP) manual 3-1.1, *General Planning and Employment Considerations* (Secret).

Finally, *the JAOP should establish guidelines for dynamic, especially time-sensitive, targeting.* Dynamic targeting is one of the most labor-intensive and intellectually demanding challenges the air and space component faces. Anticipating as much of the challenge as possible and spelling out guidance and priorities in the JAOP will ease the burden on commanders and CAOC Combat Operations Division (COD) personnel once the daily battle rhythm begins. This may prevent mistakes from being made during employment or may at least mitigate their impact. Planners should address as broad a scope as possible in as much detail as time and planning resources allow. This should include robust ROE and related legal considerations (see Appendix A).

THE TASKING CYCLE AND DELIBERATE TARGETING

Deliberate targeting provides a systematic analytical approach that focuses targeting efforts on supporting operational requirements and the commander's objectives. It helps focus the appropriate capabilities against adversary targets at the right time and place to impose specific desired effects that achieve joint force objectives. *Deliberate targeting supports the air tasking cycle, which creates a daily articulation of the overall air and space strategy. Deliberate targeting within the tasking cycle is the means Airmen use to accomplish the CFACC's non-dynamic targeting*

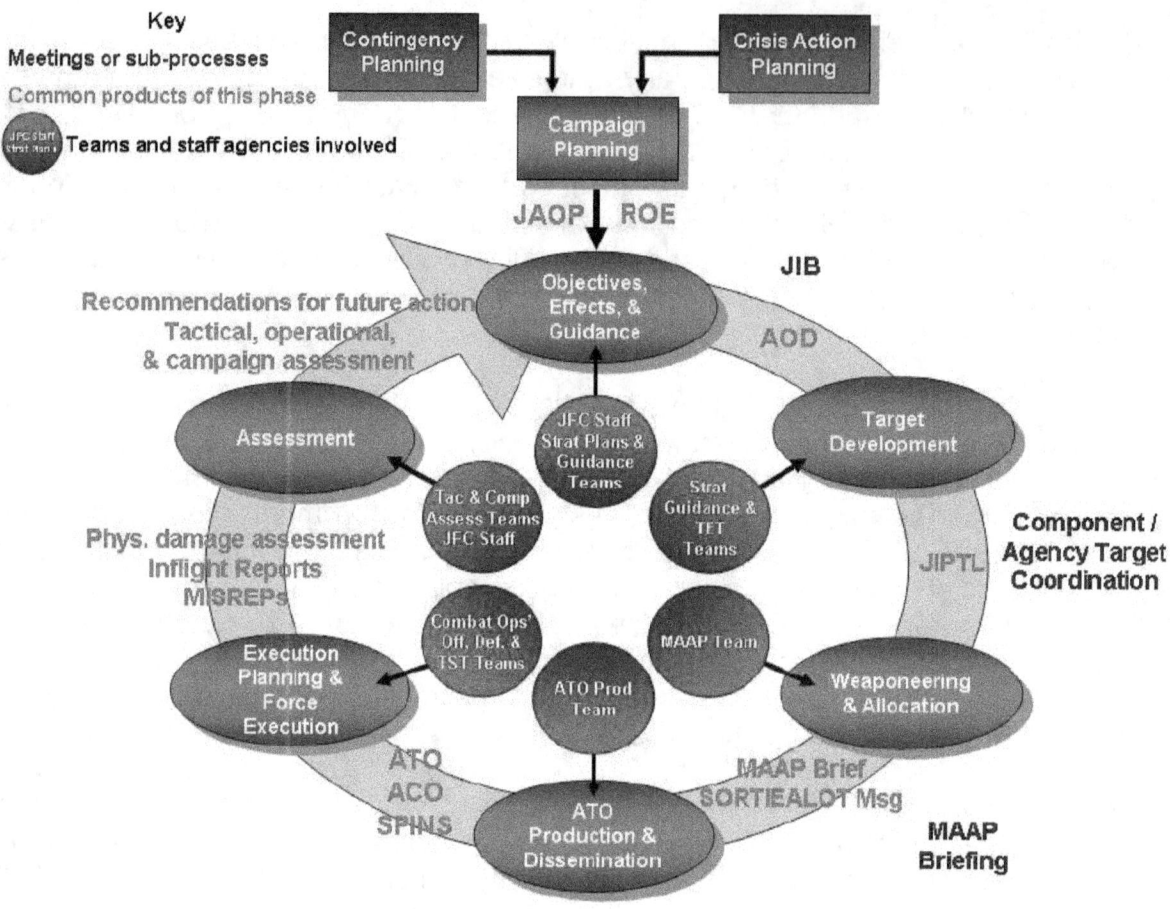

Figure 2.2. The Air Tasking Cycle

requirements. Therefore, this section discusses deliberate targeting within the context of the tasking cycle. The tasking cycle develops the products needed to build and execute an ATO and accomplish assessment. Although it is presented below as six separate, sequential phases, in reality *the targeting process is bi-directional, iterative, multi-dimensional, sometimes executed in parallel, and part of a larger set of processes.* It is built on a foundation laid by thorough IPB. Participants from the CAOC's strategy, ISR, plans, and operations divisions accomplish various targeting responsibilities, integrating their products into all levels and stages of the tasking process. The cycle consists of the following phases performed at various levels of command (see Figure 2.2):

✪ Objectives, effects, and guidance.

✪ Target development.

✪ Weaponeering and allocation.

✪ ATO production and dissemination.

✪ Execution planning and force execution.

✪ Assessment.

The tasking cycle has usually been represented as a set of distinct processes that separately accomplish targeting, apportion and allocate joint air capabilities, and produce the ATO. In fact, these processes are all closely interrelated aspects of the larger, overarching joint operation planning and execution system that is integrated throughout the campaign by the CFC. Regarding them as distinct entities misses the central insight that they must work together as an integrated whole if targeting and tasking are to be most effective. *Targeting and ATO production are essential to the tasking cycle. Although the targeting and tasking cycles perform separate and distinct functions, they are highly intertwined and require close coordination between them* and they run almost exactly in parallel once a daily battle rhythm is established. The tasking cycle as a whole encompasses the entire process of taking commanders' intent and guidance, determining where to apply force or other actions to fulfill that intent, matching available capabilities and forces with targets, putting this information into an integrated, synchronized, and coordinated order, distributing that order to all users, monitoring execution of the order to adapt to changes in the battlespace, and assessing the results of that execution. The cycle is built around finite time periods that are required to plan, integrate and coordinate, prepare for, conduct, and assess air operations. These time periods may vary from theater to theater and much targeting effort may not be bound specifically to the cycle's timeframe, but *the tasking cycle and its constituent processes drive the CAOC's battle rhythm and thus helps determine deadlines and milestones for related processes, including targeting.*

A principal purpose of the tasking cycle is to produce orders and supporting documentation to place a flexible array of capabilities in a position to create desired effects in support of the CFC's campaign. This cycle is driven by the tyranny of time and distance. It takes time for ground crew to prepare aircraft for flight, for aircrew to plan missions, and for aircrew to fly to the immediate theater of operations from distant airfields. Likewise, commanders must have enough visibility on future operations to ensure sufficient assets and crews are available to prepare for and perform tasked missions. These requirements drive the execution of a periodic, repeatable tasking process to allow commanders to plan for upcoming operations. The ATO (usually 24 hours in duration) and the process that develops it (usually 72-96 hours in duration) are a direct consequence of these physical constraints.

In contrast to the misperception that targeting information must be provided to the CFACC 72-96 hours in advance to allow targets to be struck by air assets, targets can actually be struck in minutes from when information is made available in the dynamic targeting process. The key to both the flexibility and versatility of deliberate *and* dynamic targeting is a shared understanding among the functional components of anticipated air, land, maritime and information operations during the period of the air plan. Misperceptions also arise because other components may not have visibility on the wide variety of missions tasked to the air component in support of the CFC's campaign and because air assets are often tasked to simultaneously conduct missions supporting overlapping campaign phases.

The ATO articulates tasking for joint air and space operations for a specific period of time, normally 24 hours. Detailed planning generally begins 72 hours prior the start of execution to properly assess the progress of operations, anticipate enemy actions, make needed adjustments to strategy, and enable integration of all components' requirements. The actual length of the tasking cycle may vary from theater to theater. Length will be based upon CFC guidance, CFACC direction, and theater needs. The length should be specified in theater standard operating procedures or other directives. If it is modified for a particular contingency, this should be specified in the CFC's operations plan (OPLAN) or the CFACC's JAOP. The net result of this part of the tasking cycle—and of deliberate targeting efforts—is that there are usually five ATOs in various stages of progress at any one time. (This is illustrated in figure 2.3.)

- At least one ATO undergoing assessment at various levels.
- One currently being executed.
- One in production.
- One in detailed planning (target development and weaponeering).
- One in strategy development (objectives and guidance).

Some assets may not operate within the established cycle. These include most space assets, which are tasked via the space tasking order, although some theater-specific space operations will probably be included in the daily ATO for the sake of situational awareness, integration, and synchronization. Special operations function within a 96-hour planning cycle, but will more often operate within or drive the dynamic targeting process. Certain information operations (IO) capabilities operate within a 96-hour cycle as well, and it is critical for CAOC planners to know if special operations forces (SOF) and IO personnel will assist with targeting. Intertheater air mobility assets are others that do not necessarily operate within the tasking cycle. In large operations, the existence of differing planning cycles among components can lead to increased complexity in the process. Most component planning cycles are approximately 72-96 hours. However, the requirement within the air tasking cycle to manage as many as five separate ATOs drives the requirement for discipline to manage defined inputs and outputs during particular slices of time.

The CAOC combat plans division (CPD) should work closely with the air mobility division (AMD) to determine how intertheater mobility is integrated into the ATO. Some long-range combat assets based outside the theater of operations but operating within the joint operations area may be airborne on a tasked mission before the ATO that covers their weapons' times over target is published. These assets require the most current draft ATO information and all updates that affect their missions. Other missions that are not under the CFACC's control may be included in the ATO to provide visibility and assist coordination and deconfliction.

Deliberate targeting supports every phase of the joint air estimate process and the air tasking cycle and is interwoven throughout the phases up to and including ATO production and dissemination. Effective deliberate targeting comes at a high cost in terms of the volume and flow of information. Targeting and assessment, which are integrally related, impose most of the intelligence collection burden the joint force carries—to support deliberate targeting efforts before, dynamic targeting efforts during, and assessment during and after ATO execution. Successful targeting requires in-depth information on such things as enemy force posture, capabilities, and movement; target vulnerability; enemy leadership's intentions, habits, and movement patterns; the flow and interconnections of enemy economic behavior; and the linkages and interconnections within major infrastructure systems like electrical power and electronic communications webs. The process also takes into account such things as friendly objectives, CONOPS, ROE, target time constraints, and friendly force capabilities to create five general types of products:

○ Target nomination lists that achieve desired effects in order to meet commander's objectives, guidance, and intent.

○ Weapons recommendations based upon effects chosen to achieve commander's objectives.

○ Weaponeering analyses to support effects-based kinetic and non-kinetic weapon recommendations.

○ Force / capabilities selection and planning.

○ Target materials, built to support current and future targeting efforts.

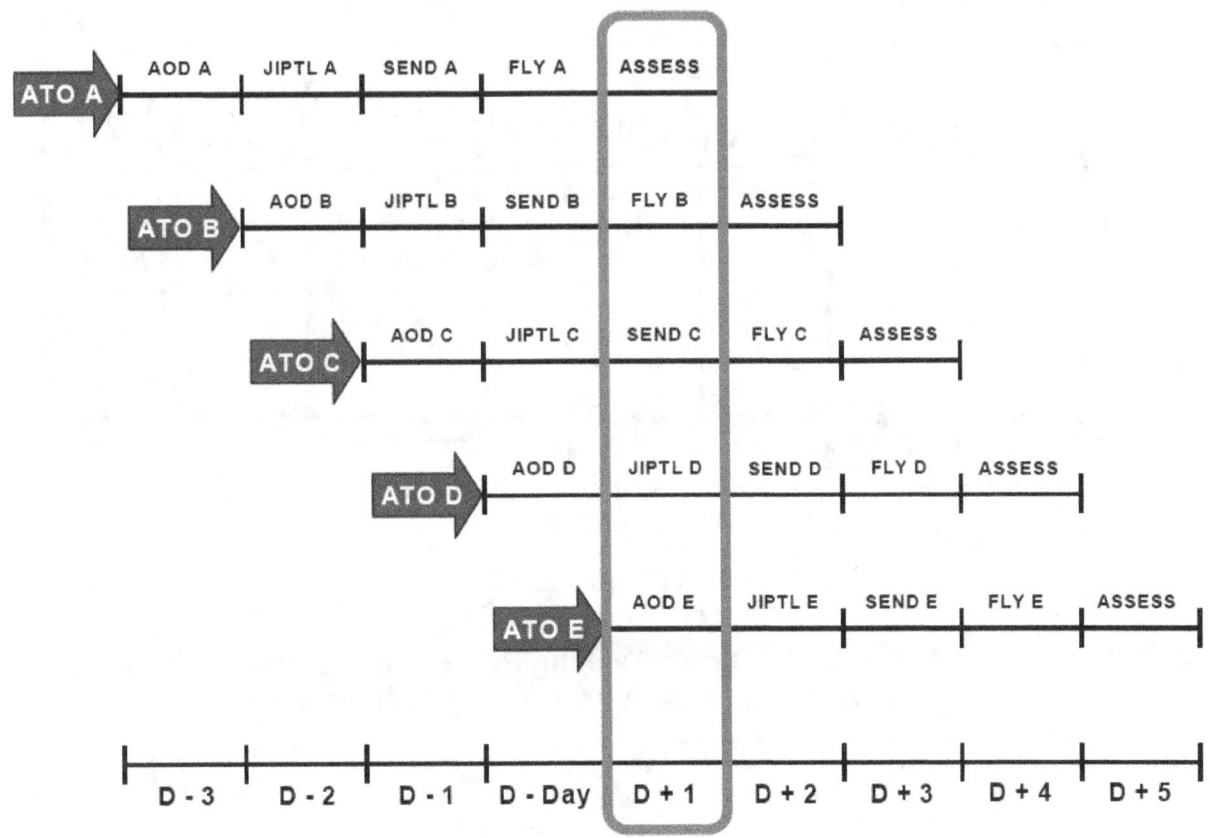

Figure 2.3. Notional CAOC Battle Rhythm with Multiple ATOs

27

The discussion in this chapter concentrates on that part of the tasking cycle that culminates in production and dissemination of the ATO. This process resides primarily in the CAOC's strategy, combat plans, and ISR divisions. Once the ATO is published, adjustments are made in the COD and targeting decisions are handled through dynamic targeting. Refer to Chapter Three for details. The final phase of the cycle is assessment, which may be less wedded to the battle rhythm's timeline than the other phases. It is accomplished primarily by the ISR division and the operational assessment team (OAT) within the strategy division (SD). Assessment is covered in Chapter Four. See Figure 2.4 for notional tasking process milestones.

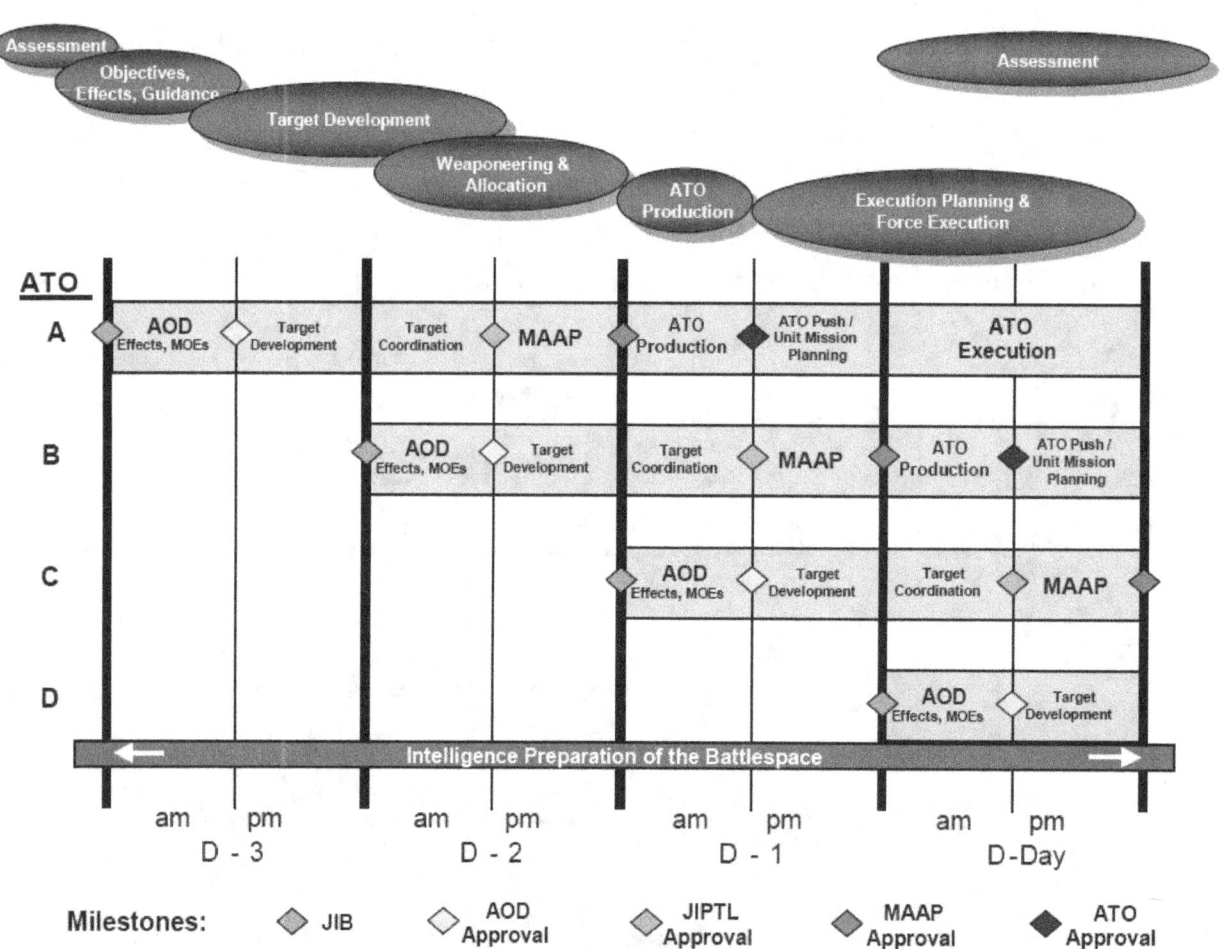

Figure 2.4. Notional Tasking Process Milestones Showing Relationship to Tasking Cycle Phases

AIR TASKING CYCLE PHASES AND THEIR PRODUCTS

Objectives, Effects, and Guidance

Purpose of the Phase

Clear understanding of the commander's objectives and guidance is essential for effective tasking and targeting. As mentioned in Chapter One, *objectives* are the clearly defined, decisive, attainable, and measurable goals toward which every military operation should be directed. They provide focus for those at all stages of the tasking cycle and give targeting personnel the overarching purpose for their efforts. *Guidance* sets limits and boundaries on the objectives and how they are attained. It establishes constraints—things we must do—and restraints—things we must *not* do. Together, the two embody a commander's intent for military operations.

This phase starts with CFC guidance to the joint force components. The CFC consults with his component commanders, decides on modifications to their COAs or schemes of maneuver, and issues guidance and intent. This has been done in various ways in different conflicts, but an emerging best practice is that used during Operation IRAQI FREEDOM (OIF) by the CFC. He established a single board to provide a forum for review of campaign progress, his intent, component schemes of maneuver, and macro-level targeting priorities.

The overarching purpose of this board is to *integrate* (not just synchronize and coordinate) component efforts at the operational, scheme-of-maneuver level. The board can thus be called a joint integration board (JIB) or a combined integration board (CIB). This board would replace and expand the scope of the joint targeting coordination board (JTCB), established as an option in joint doctrine. The J/CIB would occur earlier in the cycle and focus more at the operational, "scheme of maneuver" level than the JTCB. The CFC determines whether a J/CIB will be held and defines its role. In general, however, each J/CIB should cover four broad topics:

✪ Assessment of campaign progress since the last meeting (usually the last 24 hours), with recommendations for future action.

✪ Broad guidance for the next 72 hours issued by the CFC.

✪ Major operations (schemes of maneuver) over the next 48 hours, briefed by each of the components.

✪ Macro-level review and guidance on joint maneuver and fires (including especially targeting and ISR priorities) over the next 24 hours, to help guide joint dynamic targeting efforts for the upcoming execution period.

The CFC will normally *delegate the authority to conduct execution planning, coordination, and deconfliction associated with joint air targeting to the CFACC and will ensure that this process is a joint effort.* The CFACC must possess a sufficient command and control (C2) infrastructure, adequate facilities, and ready availability of joint planning expertise. A targeting mechanism tasked with detailed planning, weaponeering, and execution is also required to facilitate the process.

The CFACC should prepare prior to the J/CIB by consulting with senior component liaisons and the staff to determine what modifications are needed to the air scheme of maneuver and to determine the air apportionment recommendation for the CFC's approval. Air apportionment is the determination and assignment of total expected effort by percentage and/or by priority that should be devoted to the various air operations for a given period of time. Once battle rhythm starts, that period is usually 24 hours. The apportionment recommendation can be approved as part of the JIB or separately after it. Once approved, the apportionment decision should be included in the ultimate product of this phase, the AOD. In deriving guidance to be considered at the JIB and published in the AOD, the CFACC is supported by the CAOC SD's strategy plans and strategy guidance teams. The strategy guidance team is primarily responsible for producing the AOD.

The JIB may be supplemented by a joint or combined effects working group (J/CEWG) and a joint or combined assessment working group (J/CAWG), which will seek to resolve targeting and effects planning, coordination, and deconfliction at the action-officer level. The J/CEWG and J/CAWG are not standing bodies, rather they are scheduled meetings of selected elements from all components with an input to targeting, intended to ensure coordination at the lowest effective level. The J/CEWG and J/CAWG coordinate, monitor, and integrate efforts to ensure desired effects are being created in the OE, that undesired effects are mitigated, and that targeting and assessment efforts are appropriate to ensure mission success. *The J/CEWG and the J/CAWG are the appropriate fora for vetting particular issues that arise in coordinating and deconflicting individual targeting decisions.*

The objectives, effects, and guidance phase is also where effects and their accompanying measures of effect (MOE) and measures of performance (MOP) are determined. Strategy guidance and strategy plans teams work closely with the CPD Targeting Effects Team (TET), (formerly known as the guidance, apportionment, and targeting [GAT] Team) and the ISR division (ISRD) to determine effects that achieve the stated objectives, select appropriate measures and indicators for assessment, and determine ISR requirements to collect against the MOEs. Results of this effort may be published as lists of tasks or desired effects in the AOD.

Finally, considerations of the LOAC and ROE for the conflict will directly affect all phases of the tasking process (and thus targeting). Targeteers must understand and be able to apply the basic principles of these disciplines as they relate to targeting. See Appendix A for further discussion of LOAC and ROE.

Products of the Phase

The Air and Space Operations Directive. The CAOC strategy division drafts the AOD for CFACC approval. In a normal battle rhythm, this is done on a daily basis. The

AOD is the vehicle for the CFACC to express his intent for a specific day and communicate the CFC's apportionment decision. Apportionment guidance should reflect prioritized operational objectives and relevant tactical tasks with approximate weights of effort for each objective. Specific weights of effort should be avoided due to the difficulty in precisely measuring effects of air, space, and IO, and to allow maximum flexibility in planning the application of airpower. However the CPD can use these weights of effort, along with existing friendly force capabilities, to estimate the numbers of aimpoints by effect or objective to focus target development. (See Air Force Operational Tactics, Techniques, And Procedures [AFOTTP] manual 2-3.2, *Air and Space Operations Center*, for an AOD sample).

The prioritized tasks in the AOD should be effects-based and reflect commander's guidance and intent. By crafting effects-based tasks for the AOD, target developers within the CAOC's ISRD gain the flexibility to identify and nominate the most effective means to achieve the desired effects. Tasks that are not effects-based are often target-based, meaning that there is little flexibility in the selection of targets, and can lead to the inefficient use of scarce air and space resources. *The AOD is the primary vehicle for communicating desired effects to target developers and others involved in targeting on a daily basis.* Robust, logical lists of effects-based tasks with appropriate MOEs and ISR collection requirements are a necessary part of the AOD.

The AOD should also be used to express the CFC's and CFACC's guidance regarding what target categories (target sets) are time-sensitive targets, what the priority is among them, and what types of dynamic targeting would cause preplanned missions to be re-tasked. Categories of TST, high-value targets, and other objects of dynamic targeting should be presented in the context of the desired effects, and those desired effects prioritized against the desired effects for preplanned targets. This allows the COD to rapidly assess the value of preplanned targets against TST or emerging targets to determine whether or not to re-task air, space, or information assets. This guidance also reduces the possibility of all newly detected targets being struck. Just because a target can be engaged within the ATO execution period does not mean that effort should be diverted from preplanned targets to engage it.

While daily guidance is critical to subsequent phases of the ongoing tasking cycle, the SD strategy plans team also works on longer-range planning, including study of branches and sequels. Conclusions drawn from this study should be disseminated throughout the CAOC to assist in focusing later target development and intelligence collection efforts.

Finally, the AOD should include the CFACC's guidance on which targets or target sets require immediate assessment feedback. ISR collection assets are usually limited in number and the collection requirements for target development, IPB, indications and warnings, and other taskings may have a higher priority than tactical assessment. Operations will be more efficient if tactical assessment is focused on a select few high priority targets or sets.

Target Development

Purpose of the Phase

This is the phase in which the efforts of deliberate targeting relate specific targets to objectives, desired effects, and accompanying actions. Targeteers within the ISRD and the CPD TET take the effects determined during the objectives, effects, and guidance phase and analyze which targets must be struck (or otherwise affected) to accomplish them. Target development requires thorough examination of the adversary as a system of systems in order to understand where critical linkages and vulnerabilities lie. Critical things are those a system requires in order to function. Critical linkages within a system often enable the functioning of several interrelated parts of the system, and so affecting them in the right way can disable several components or even cause cascading system-wide failure. Vulnerable things are those that can be attacked or otherwise affected with relative ease. Thorough analysis should reveal "critical vulnerabilities," if they exist. These are elements of the adversary's system that are both critical and vulnerable. Analysis is made effective through access to the greatest possible breadth of subject matter expertise and information regarding the functioning of systems that support adversary behavior. This research will require expertise beyond that normally available on the CFACC's planning staff. It requires cooperation with other planning staffs and national interagency groups throughout the process. Much of the required analysis is done before conflict begins. See Chapter Five and Appendix B for further details.

Target development involves five distinct functions, each discussed below:

- ✪ Target analysis.
- ✪ Target vetting.
- ✪ Target validation.
- ✪ Target nomination.
- ✪ Collection and exploitation requirements.

The purpose of these together is to relate target development to tasking. The target nomination part of the process usually culminates in a target coordination meeting, held by the TET within the CPD, with the assistance of the various joint components and multi-national liaison elements. The TET collates target nominations from all sources. It works with the ISRD and other agencies to analyze targets. It screens all nominated targets to ensure they meet commander's intent and are relevant. It allocates and prioritizes the nominated targets based on the best potential to achieve desired effects and objectives and coordinates this target allocation to ensure other components' priorities and timing requirements are met. The product of this effort, when approved by the CFC or designated representative, is the JIPTL.

There are no absolutes in target development or its relation to the larger tasking cycle. As noted, all the phases of the tasking process are intertwined. Target development efforts can frequently force refinement of desired effects or even objectives, especially if weaponeering and allocation efforts indicate that a particular targeting avenue of approach is impractical. Target development efforts also frequently reach forward to influence weaponeering and allocation choices, dynamic targeting during execution, and the assessment process. The results of detailed target development are often stored in target system studies, individual target folders and targeting databases that can be studied by all levels of command and used in future target development efforts.

Target Analysis takes the desired effects determined during planning or the first phase of the tasking cycle and matches them to specific targets. This analysis looks at the importance of various potential targets as enablers of enemy capabilities, as critical elements within enemy systems, or as potential trigger points for desired enemy behavior changes. There are many means available to accomplish this. Two of the most common that have been used in the past are target system and critical node analysis.

Target system analysis (TSA), as its name implies, approaches targets and target sets as systems to determine vulnerabilities and exploitable weaknesses. Targeteers review how a functional target system works as a whole and analyze the interactions between components. TSA takes a system-of-systems approach to look at interdependencies and vulnerabilities between systems as well as intra-system dependencies in order to maximize the effectiveness of target development. TSA begins in peacetime, before the commencement of conflict, and is accomplished with federated support and "reachback" (see Chapter Five and Appendix B).

As part of a comprehensive system-of-systems analysis (SOSA) approach, TSA focuses on one or more of the many "functional target systems" identified in Defense Intelligence Agency (DIA) handbooks within a particular theater, such as infrastructure targets across a whole region or nation (like electrical power or petroleum, oil, and lubricants [POL] production), or non-infrastructure systems such as financial networks. SOSA seeks to find nodes common to more than one system, focusing on the interactions and interrelationships between system elements, in order to determine their degree and points of interdependence and to discern linkages between their functions. The ultimate goal of TSA is to find critical nodes and vulnerabilities that, if disrupted or affected in a specific manner, create effects that achieve the commander's objectives.

The analysis performed in target development proceeds through successively greater levels of detail, flowing from the macro (broad scope) level to the micro (narrowly focused) level. This winnowing approach is essential to preserve the linkage between desired effects and objectives and the specific actions that are taken against particular targets. It determines the necessary type, breadth, and duration of action that must be exerted on each target to generate effects that are consistent with the commander's objectives.

Targets for consideration come from a variety of sources. Many are developed pre-conflict and confirmed during planning. These may or may not come from a theater joint target list (JTL) maintained in peacetime. JTLs are consolidated lists of selected targets considered to have military significance in a combatant commander's area of responsibility. Many more are suggested during JAOP development or by the SD as the air and space component's strategy evolves during a conflict. Many are derived by the CAOC's targeteers themselves, as target analysis suggests the means of achieving desired effects.

Many targets are nominated by other joint force components in order to help achieve their desired effects. Upon dissemination of the AOD, and based on CFC guidance, components begin to develop their nominations for inclusion in the next ATO. Some targets may be suggested by government agencies outside the DOD or by foreign governments. The product of target analysis is a list of proposed target nominations designed to achieve the effects determined in earlier stages of planning (such as JAOP development or the objectives, effect, and guidance stage of the tasking cycle), which will then be validated. Other products may include creation of or additions to no-strike or restricted target lists (see "products of the phase," below).

Target research within the tasking cycle often entails studying previously unidentified or unlocated targets. Responsibility for the research lies primarily, but not solely, with the ISRD, which uses federated aid and reachback (see Chapter Five and Appendix B) to ensure that the CAOC obtains, analyzes, and disseminates the information it needs for further target development. The CAOC's information warfare element may also be crucial to target research, especially in helping understand battlespace communications and intelligence systems as well as human factors.

Much ISRD effort must also be put into determining the status of previously struck targets, enemy recovery and recuperation efforts, and changes in enemy tactics, processes, and strategy. This information is critical in validating the effectiveness of friendly action. It helps shape ongoing target development within the tasking cycle by showing where re-strikes or other further action may be required. It is also crucial to the SD's efforts to identify needed changes in the overall air and space strategy.

Target vetting leverages the expertise of the national intelligence community to verify the accuracy and fidelity of the intelligence and analysis used to develop the target. Additionally, vetting reviews individual targets' compliance with the LOAC and ROE. See Appendix A for further discussion of LOAC and ROE requirements.

Target validation ensures all vetted targets achieve the effects and objectives outlined in a commander's guidance and are coordinated and deconflicted with agencies and activities that might present a conflict with the proposed action. It also determines whether a target remains a viable element of the target system. During the development effort, the targets may also require review and approval based on the sensitive target approval and review process, coordinated through the combatant commander to national authorities. This phase is done by targeteers within the CPD

TET, in consultation with the strategy plans team within the SD and other experts and agencies, as required. The first part of validation asks such questions as:

- ✪ Does the target meet CFACC or higher commanders' objectives, guidance, and intent?

- ✪ Is the target consistent with LOAC and ROE?

- ✪ Is the desired effect on the target consistent with the end state?

- ✪ Is the target politically or culturally "sensitive?"

  - ✪✪ What will the effect of striking it be on public opinion (enemy, friendly, and neutral)?

- ✪ What are the risks and likely consequences of collateral damage?

- ✪ Is it feasible to attack this target? What is the risk?

- ✪ Is it feasible to attack the target *at this time*?

- ✪ What are the consequences of *not* attacking the target?

- ✪ Will attacking the target negatively affect friendly operations due to current or planned friendly exploitation of the target?

The second part of validation starts the coordination and integration of actions against the target with other operations. This continues after the ATO is produced and responsibility is assumed by the COD. Part of coordination is deconfliction, which is largely a checklist function. The checklist should be developed during JAOP development and be appropriate to the particular organization and conflict. Many offices and agencies must be coordinated with to prevent fratricide, collateral damage, or propaganda leverage for the enemy. Some examples of where coordination and integration are required:

- ✪ SOF. The joint forces special operations component commander (JFSOCC) must deconflict joint special operations with the CFC and the other component commanders to avoid fratricide. This is best done at a CFACC targeting coordination meeting held as part of the TET's function. The CAOC should work through the special operations liaison element (SOLE) for deconfliction.

- ✪ Army forces. CAOC personnel should work through the BCD within the CAOC and the ASOC to ensure that air and space component targeting is coordinated and integrated with land component operations. Careful crafting and placement of FSCM facilitate this.

- ✪ Search and rescue.

- ✪ Information operations.

- ✪ Other government agencies.

The first three stages result in what might be called "target allocation"—working interactively with other elements in the CAOC to determine which targets "make the cut" on the given day's ATO. This is not always an easy decision, especially in conflicts where resources are limited and/or the target lists are lengthy. Still, it is a vital part of what the CPD does. The final stage produces a list of validated target nominations that will be submitted to higher authority for approval on target nomination lists.

...the nature of warfare has changed. When cities were struck in past wars, none doubted that civilians, embassies, hospitals, and schools would be in harm's way. Today, our ability to strike precisely has created the impression that sensitive sites can be safe in the middle of a war zone. Our desire to protect innocents in the line of fire has added an enormous burden on all of us that we accept. It is our job to do our best to ensure that only appropriate targets be struck.

—George Tenet
Former Director of Central Intelligence (DCI)
Remarks to the House Permanent Select Committee on Intelligence, 22

Target Nomination. Once targets are identified and validated, they are nominated through proper channels for approval. Historically, this has often entailed deliberation through a high-level coordinating body such as a JTCB, but evolving best practice (including practice in OIF) suggests that detailed targeting functions should be delegated to components (as joint doctrine permits), leaving commanders free to concentrate on integrating the joint force scheme of maneuver in a JIB.

Once all of the component, allied, and agency target nominations for a given ATO are received, the TET prioritizes the nominated targets and places them in a target nomination list (TNL) based on the commander's objectives. The TET then vets the TNLs through the appropriate coordinating bodies representing the joint force components and other required agencies to ensure their requirements are supported, joint force priorities are met, and desired effects are achieved.

If targeting functions are delegated appropriately, the final deconfliction and coordination of components' nominations should be at a target coordination meeting run by the TET. Component representatives should be prepared to justify target selections, since not all targets may be struck based on the CFC's apportionment decision and the CFACC's target allocation. If differences arise and cannot be resolved at the meeting, the issue should be coordinated at higher levels for resolution. The meeting should not generally address mating of specific weapons to targets, but it should consider non-kinetic options and initiate the planning and coordination needed for those options. Additionally, the meeting may address the availability of certain "high demand" weapons or munitions on a particular ATO. However, the availability of weapons or capability should not drive the nomination of targets—this is antithetical to an effects-based approach.

The result of coordination is the JIPTL, which is submitted to the CFC or designated representative for approval. Again, targets may be added to no-strike or restricted target lists as a result of this part of the process, too.

Determining collection and exploitation requirements through assessment is critical to targeting efforts. This stage attempts to answer the question, "how will we know we've achieved the desired effects?" by establishing intelligence collection and exploitation requirements for each nominated target. This stage begins with target analysis and runs parallel to the other stages. The requirements must be articulated early in the tasking process to support target development and ultimately assessment. Targeteers must work closely with collection managers to ensure that target development, pre-strike, and post-strike requirements are integrated into the collection plan, along with any changes that occur throughout the tasking cycle. This intelligence support is also required to prepare for future targeting during execution (e.g., to pre-task real time ISR assets) and to support post-strike assessment of success. Properly identifying collection and exploitation requirements is one of the keys to effective PBA. The product of this stage may be a joint integrated prioritized collection list (JIPCL).

Products of the Phase

The JIPTL is a prioritized list of targets and associated data approved by the CFC or designated representative and maintained by the joint force. An approved JIPTL is the central product of the target development phase. Targets and priorities are derived from the recommendations of components in conjunction with their proposed operations supporting the CFC's objectives and guidance. Although it draws from many sources, the CPD TET has primary responsibility for the JIPTL within the CAOC.

The JIPCL is a prioritized list of intelligence collection and exploitation requirements needed to support indications and warning, analysis, and future target development efforts and to measure whether desired effects and objectives are being achieved. Requirements and priorities are derived from the recommendations of components in conjunction with their proposed operations supporting the CFC's objectives and guidance. An approved JIPCL may be a product of answering information gaps as well as the collection and exploitation requirements stage of target development. The ISRD has primary responsibility within the CAOC for the JIPCL, although considerable consultation with the SD OAT is required.

The no strike list (NSL) is a list of geographic areas, complexes, installations, forces, equipment, capabilities, functions, individuals, groups, systems, or behaviors that will not have action planned against them Attacking these may violate LOAC or interfere with friendly relations with indigenous personnel or governments. Combatant commanders and JFCs determine which targets are included on the NSL based upon inputs from components, supporting unified commands, or higher authorities. Targets on this list require national-level approval to strike.

The restricted target list is a list of targets that have specific restrictions imposed upon them. Actions on restricted targets are prohibited until coordinated and approved by the establishing headquarters. Targets are restricted because certain types of actions against them may have negative political, cultural, or propaganda implications, or may interfere with projected friendly operations. The RTL is nominated by elements of the joint force and approved by the CFC. Targets on this list may only be struck with CFC or higher approval. This list also includes restricted targets directed by higher authorities. Actions taken by an opponent may remove a target from the RTL.

The CFC's staff develops and maintains the NSL and RTL. The components recommend changes to it during peacetime, while the J-2 is developing the JTL, and during conflict.

Weaponeering and Allocation

Purpose of the Phase

Weaponeering is the part of the tasking process for estimating the quantity and types of lethal and non-lethal weapons needed to achieve desired effects against specific targets. (Note: This modifies the joint definition found in JP 1-02.) Allocation, in the broadest sense, is the distribution of limited resources among competing requirements for employment. This has two aspects that are relevant to the air tasking cycle: allocation of targets and allocation of forces. Weaponeering and allocation function together to produce the master air attack plan (MAAP); see "products of the phase," below. These efforts also commence before the JIPTL is approved and continue past MAAP production into execution planning. They are integral to all of targeting.

Weaponeering considers such things as the desired effects against the target (both direct weapons effects and indirect desired outcomes), target vulnerability, delivery accuracy, damage criteria, and weapon reliability. Targeteers quantify the expected results of lethal and non-lethal weapons employment against prioritized targets to produce desired effects. It results in probable outcomes given many replications of an event. It does not predict the outcome of every munition delivery, but represents statistical averages based on modeling, weapons tests, and real-world experience. With modern precision and near-precision weapons, however, the probabilities of accurate delivery and of achieving intended direct effects are very high and are still increasing. Weaponeering is normally done by the ISRD targeting team prior to TET using methodologies prepared by the joint technical coordinating group for munition effectiveness and data found in the joint munitions effectiveness manuals (JMEM). The final weaponeering is chosen by the MAAP Team. The output of weaponeering is a recommendation of the quantity, type, and mix of lethal and non-lethal weapons needed to achieve desired effects while avoiding unacceptable collateral damage. All approved targets are weaponeered to include at least the following:

- ✪ Target identification and description.
- ✪ Recommended aim points/DPIs.
- ✪ Desired level(s) of damage, degradation, or exploitation.
- ✪ Weapon system and munitions recommendations.
- ✪ Fuzing requirements (if required).
- ✪ Probability of achieving desired direct effect(s).
- ✪ Target area terrain, weather, and threat considerations.
- ✪ Collateral damage considerations.
- ✪ WMD agent dispersal / collateral effects.

Precautions must be taken to avoid or minimize civilian casualties and damage to civilian infrastructure. The danger of collateral damage varies with the type of target, terrain, weapons used, weather, and the proximity of civilians and their structures. According to LOAC, incidental damage to civilian objects must not be excessive in relation to the expected military advantage to be gained. If an attack is directed against dual-use objects that might be legitimate military targets but also serve a legitimate civilian need (e.g., electrical power or telecommunications), then this factor must be carefully balanced against the military benefits when making a weapons selection, as must reconstruction and stabilization considerations following the end of hostilities. Thus, those conducting weaponeering must always keep campaign objectives and the end state in mind, as must those in other CAOC teams and divisions who review weaponeering solutions and the MAAP. The methodologies and data used for weaponeering analyses are also capable of producing estimations of collateral damage risk to noncombatants and non-targeted facilities. Established ROE and LOAC also address collateral damage concerns. (See Appendix A for further information.) Targeteers must comply with Joint Chiefs of Staff CD estimation methodology. For example, it may sometimes be necessary to strike a target more precisely than would otherwise be necessary in order to avoid collateral civilian damage. Certain levels of collateral damage estimation require expertise that lies outside of the CFACC's—or even CFC's—control and must be coordinated through the ISRD via federated and reachback relationships.

In another sense, the very precision of certain weaponeering solutions, especially against some hardened and/or buried targets, may cause ripple effects through other CAOC divisions or joint agencies because intended effects may not be readily visible. This happened during DESERT STORM, when Iraqi hardened aircraft shelters were repeatedly struck because the results of earlier fully effective attacks were not immediately apparent.

It is critically important to stress that all estimates generated during this phase are situation-specific, reflecting the pairing of a particular force against a particular target, under a particular condition of employment. As such, users of this information should be cautioned against assuming that the estimated effectiveness of a force capability under one set of circumstances is broadly applicable to other circumstances. Relatively minor targeting variations may have an exaggerated impact on effects estimates. It is equally important to stress these estimates of performance are not designed to take into account considerations outside of the realm of weapon-target interaction (e.g., they do not address whether or not the delivery system will survive to reach the target.)

Targeteers must know the capabilities of platforms, weapons, and fuzes for kinetic weapons available for use and be aware of their availability. They must also be familiar with the standard conventional load platforms in their theater and delivery tactics. Weaponeering results will only be useful if the employment parameters assumed in weaponeering match those used in combat. Targeteers should work closely with the operations and logistics staff to obtain required information. As a rule of thumb, theater component targeting branches should request a copy of the time-phased force and deployment data (TPFDD) to obtain units' expected input options selected from the JMEM's automated programs, to provide realistic planning data. Weaponeering must also take into account the availability of the various weapons being considered. Certain high value weapons, such as those capable of deep penetration or other special effects, are normally limited in number and should only be used against those targets that both require the weapon for successful attack and are of sufficiently high priority to warrant the expenditure of the resource. Making these decisions is part of "target allocation." Finally, some weapons, particularly certain IO capabilities, require long lead times in planning, deployment, and approval, which means that such capabilities must be thought about early and included in the JAEP.

Allocation. As mentioned previously, there are two types of allocation relevant to the tasking cycle. The first is "target allocation" and it starts early in the targeting process. Prior to the TET target coordination meeting, the MAAP team determines how many aimpoints can be serviced on the given ATO day from the MAAP Team. The TET then goes over the lists of nominated targets and determines which "make the cut" on that day's proposed JIPTL. The TET must work closely with the SD and the MAAP team to ensure the prioritized list ties into the JAOP and AOD appropriately. The SD must ensure the TET understands how effects and objectives are prioritized, how they are to be achieved over time, and that it has a macro-level idea of the number of targets associated with each objective. The TET then collects target nominations from other sources and works a daily allocation of targets that have been planned against the effects and objectives to build the daily JIPTL. Approaching JIPTL construction in this way helps avoid an ad hoc, target-servicing approach.

The second type of allocation is "force allocation" (or air allocation as it is customarily thought of). This is the translation of the air apportionment decision into the total number of sorties or missions by weapon system type available for each operation or task. (Note: This modifies the joint definition found in JP 1-02.) It falls under the

CPD MAAP team, which takes the final prioritized list of weaponeered targets and allocates airpower by melding available capabilities and resources with the TET's weaponeering recommendations. The result is a translation of the total weight of air effort into the total number or sorties or missions required to achieve desired effects.

Although not complete until the MAAP is produced, force allocation also starts early in the cycle. Each air capable joint force component submits an allocation request (ALLOREQ) message to the CFACC (timed to coincide with the beginning of the MAAP part of the tasking process, usually not later than 36 hours prior to the start of a given ATO day). ALLOREQs contain requests for air and space component support and information on sorties from other components not required for organic component support that are available for CFACC tasking. The MAAP team works with the TET through JIPTL production, then takes inputs from them, the component liaisons, the AMD (especially concerning tanker availability), and others to produce the MAAP. They determine an overall sortie flow for the ATO period and determine how that flow should be divided into "packages"—discrete sets of missions and sorties designed to complement each other or provide required support (for example, tankers and electronic warfare assets "packaged" with the strike assets they are supporting). They also determine required times over target or times on station. Packages are arranged in sequence and used to determine a timeline and resource requirements for the ATO period. Each package should be deconflicted in time, space, and effect.

Part of the allocation and MAAP portions of the tasking process is creation of an ISR and assessment plan. Theater ISR assets must be carefully orchestrated to ensure optimal coverage of the operational environment. Assets should be positioned not only to provide tactical assessment of targets planned for attack, but must be able to detect emerging targets and be flexible enough to collect against them as well. At the same time, ISR assets must continue to monitor the "bigger picture," in order to help discern whether desired effects are being created and whether the enemy is adapting his COAs to our actions. The assessment plan cannot be made in a vacuum, but must be closely coordinated with all other planning efforts.

The CAOC should establish procedures to ensure that the organizations nominating targets receive continuous feedback on the status of their nominations throughout the tasking cycle. For example, not all targets nominated will be approved for the JIPTL, nor will all targets on the JIPTL be included on the ATO. There must be a feedback mechanism to ensure that targets not attacked, for any reason, are reported to the nominating authority for consideration on future JIPTLs.

Products of the Phase

The MAAP is the CFACC's time-phased air and space scheme of maneuver for a given ATO period, synthesizing commander's guidance, desired effects, supported components' schemes of maneuver, friendly capabilities, and likely enemy COAs, and allocating friendly resources against approved targets. (Note: this modifies the joint definition found in JP 1-02) The MAAP is usually presented in the form of a decision briefing for the CFACC. The CPD MAAP team is responsible for producing the MAAP.

The sortie allotment message (SORTIEALOT) is a means by which the CFC can allot sorties to meet requirements of subordinate commanders that are expressed in their air employment and/or allocation plans. It may or may not be produced during this phase of the tasking cycle, based on availability of limited air resources and component requirements.

ATO Production and Dissemination

Purpose of the Phase

This phase finalizes the ATO and associated orders, physically produces them, and disseminates them to combat units. It is based on commanders' guidance (especially the AOD), the MAAP, and component requirements. This is accomplished by the CPD ATO production team. *Airspace control and air defense instructions must be provided in sufficient detail to allow components to plan and execute all missions listed in the ATO.* These are usually captured in the airspace control order (ACO) and the day's SPINS. These directions must enable combat operations without undue restrictions, balancing combat effectiveness with the safe, orderly, and expeditious use of airspace. Instructions must provide for quick coordination of task assignment or reassignment and must direct aircraft identification and engagement procedures and ROE appropriate to the nature of the threat. These instructions should also consider the volume of friendly air traffic, friendly air defense requirements, identification friend or foe technology, weather, and adversary capabilities. Instructions contained in the SPINS and the ACO are updated as frequently as required. The ATO, ACO, and SPINS provide operational and tactical direction at appropriate levels of detail. The level of detail should be very explicit when forces operate from different bases and multi-component and/or composite missions are tasked. By contrast, less detail is required when missions are tasked to a single component or base. Components may submit critical changes to target requests and asset availability during this phase of the cycle.

Products of the Phase

The ATO is a method used to task and disseminate to components, subordinate units, and command and control agencies projected sorties, capabilities and/or forces to targets and specific missions. It normally provides specific instructions to include call signs, targets, controlling agencies, etc., as well as general instructions. The ATO may subsume the ACO and SPINS, or these may be published as separate orders.

SPINS are a separate instruction or section of the ATO that provides information that is not otherwise available in the ATO, but is necessary for its implementation. It includes such information as commanders' guidance (often including the AOD itself), the C2 battle management plan, ROE, combat search and rescue procedures, the communications plan, general instructions for inter- and intra-theater airlift, and so on. It may also include the ACO.

The ACO provides direction to deconflict, coordinate, and integrate the use of airspace within the operational area. (Note: this does not imply any level of command authority over air assets.) It may be included as a section of or appendix to the SPINS (and thus of the ATO).

Execution Planning and Force Execution

Purpose of the Phase

Execution planning includes the preparation necessary for combat units to accomplish the decentralized execution of the ATO. It generally consists of the 12 hours immediately prior to the start of a given day's ATO execution period. Force execution refers to the 24-hour period in which a particular ATO is executed by combat units. The CAOC aids both, preparing input for, supporting, and monitoring execution. *The commander of Air Force forces (COMAFFOR), as the Air Force's warfighting commander, directs execution of Air Force air and space capabilities. If a CFACC is appointed, that commander directs execution of air and space capabilities and forces made available for joint or combined operations.* It is normal, of course, for the COMAFFOR to also be the CFACC. Inherent in this is the authority to redirect joint or combined air assets. Under the Air Force doctrine of centralized control and decentralized execution, unit commanders are given the freedom and flexibility to plan missions and delivery tactics as long as they fall within timing requirements, ROE, and intent of effects. The CFACC coordinates redirection of sorties that were previously allocated for support of component operations with affected component commanders.

During execution, the CAOC is the central agency for revising the tasking of air forces. It is also responsible for coordinating and deconflicting any changes with appropriate agencies or components. It may or may not have authority to re-direct use of space and information capabilities supporting theater efforts, depending upon the asset.

Due to battlespace dynamics, the CFACC may be required to make changes to planned operations during execution. The CAOC must be flexible and responsive to changes required during execution of the ATO. Forces not apportioned for joint or combined operations, but included on the ATO for coordination purposes, can be redirected only with the approval of the respective component or allied commanders. During execution, the CFACC is also responsible for retargeting air assets to respond to emerging targets or changing priorities. The CFACC may delegate the authority to re-direct missions made available for higher priority targets to C2 mission commanders as necessary. The CAOC must be notified of all redirected missions, however.

The COD supervises the detailed execution of the ATO. Targeteers are an integral part of combat operations. They monitor ATO execution and recommend alternate targets when necessary. Normally, targeting changes are needed due to adverse weather, assessment requirements, or modification of priorities. The ability to quickly recommend good alternate targets is very important to the flexibility of air and space power. Combat operations targeteers should be aware of all significant information for targets on the current ATO, desired effects and objectives, all guidance, ROEs, and weaponeering lookup tables as appropriate. More on this topic can be found in the next chapter.

The rational use of force relies on the capability to identify adversary entities as a precursor to taking action against them, especially if doing so entails the use of force. CID of *all* battlespace entities is thus a critical enabling capability in any use, or potential use, of military force. Identifying adversary or enemy entities is essential, of course, but so is identifying friendly and neutral entities. "Blue force tracking" (BFT) is a core function of CID. BFT is the employment of techniques to identify and track US, allied, and coalition forces for the purpose of providing commanders enhanced situational awareness and reducing fratricide. For more information on CID and BFT, see AFTTP 3-1.1 (Secret), Appendix 2.

Results and Products of the Phase

This is the phase in which targets are actually struck (or otherwise affected) and direct effects are created. Other products include physical damage assessments and MISREPs, used in helping make physical damage and other assessments.

Assessment

Purpose of the Phase

Assessment is the measure of progress in a campaign or operation, the means of telling whether desired effects are being created and objectives achieved, and of evaluating what needs to be done next. Effective planning and execution require continuing evaluation of the effectiveness of friendly and enemy action. Consequently, assessment is much more than "battle damage" or "combat assessment," as it has traditionally been presented—and more than just an intelligence function that takes place after execution has concluded. Planning for it begins prior to commencement of operations, takes place throughout planning and execution, and continues after the conflict is over. It is a central part of an effects-based approach to conflict. It consists of four distinct levels: tactical assessment (which includes assessment of physical damage), component-level operational assessment, CFC-level operational assessment, and national-level assessment. Each lower level feeds the levels above it and provides a basis for broader-based evaluation of progress. This subject is treated in detail in Chapter Four.

Products of the Phase

Products include various tactical, operational, and campaign assessment products discussed further in Chapter Four, along with recommendations for future action.

CHAPTER THREE

DYNAMIC TARGETING

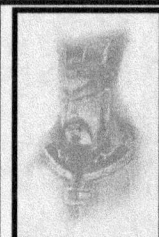 *When the strike of a hawk breaks the body of its prey, it is because of timing. Thus the momentum of one skilled in war is overwhelming and his attack prompt.*

—Sun Tzu

GENERAL

"Dynamic targeting" is a term that applies to all targeting prosecuted outside of a given day's preplanned ATO targets. It represents the targeting portion of the "execution" phase of effects-based operations. *It is essential for commanders and CAOC personnel to keep effects-based principles and the objectives in mind during dynamic targeting and ATO execution. It is easy for those caught up in the daily battle rhythm to become too focused on tactical-level details, losing sight of objectives and desired effects or other aspects of commander's intent.* When this happens, execution can devolve into blind target servicing, unguided by strategy and with little or no anticipation of enemy actions.

Dynamic targeting is different from deliberate targeting in terms of the timing of the steps in the process, but not much different in the substance of the steps. Ultimately, "dynamic" targets are targets—as such, their nomination, development, execution, and assessment still take place within the larger framework of the targeting and tasking cycles. However, all targets processed during the current execution cycle have one thing in common: they are "time-sensitive" to some degree or have increased in priority due to battlespace changes. Some, indeed, are fleeting and require near-immediate prosecution if they are to be targeted at all. Such targets require a procedure that can be worked through quickly and that facilitates quick transition from receipt of intelligence through targeting solution to action against the target. Recent operations have indicated that this compressed decision cycle is best handled through a specialized sub-process, known as the dynamic targeting procedure. Seen from the larger cycle's perspective, dynamic targeting takes place within phases five ("execution planning and force execution") and six ("assessment") of the targeting and tasking cycles. The earlier phases serve to provide commanders' targeting guidance and determine CONOPS for making the resources that will prosecute dynamic targeting available.

The combat operations division has overall responsibility for implementation of dynamic targeting. Successful dynamic targeting, however, requires a great deal of prior planning and coordination with other divisions within the CAOC and with other components. If dynamic targeting is to be done correctly, planners must develop a plan that makes assets available to the COD prior to the start of execution. This can be done in a number of ways. Among the most common methods are:

✪ Preplanned target reference methods and coordination measures such as kill boxes.

✪ "On-call" or pre-positioned strike and ISR packages (including tanker support) for rapid response to emerging targets (such as on-call air interdiction missions available for tasking during ATO execution; missions on ground alert; and/or air-to-ground weapons loaded on aircraft performing defensive counterair missions).

✪ Using IPB to determine the most probable areas where targets will emerge during execution.

✪ Diverting airborne assets assigned to lower priority targets to strike the recently identified target.

✪ Coordination and synchronization of dynamic targeting operations by streamlining procedures.

✪ Developing procedures for rapid handover of the mission tasking to another component for mission execution if the air and space component cannot attack a target that emerges.

Divisions other than the COD have important roles to play in dynamic targeting. The SD, for instance, must capture macro-level targeting guidance to include component priorities in the daily AOD. Many items in the AOD, like commander's intent, anticipated weapons available, ROE, acceptable risk levels, and elements of the ISR collection plan, may be vital. ROE are especially important to this form of time-compressed targeting. While the SD typically drafts ROE inputs with advice from the judge advocate (JA), all involved in planning and execution must clearly understand the ROE. Compliance with ROE is a shared responsibility between the CFACC staff, subordinate command elements, and aircrews/operators. Due to the time-sensitive nature of targets prosecuted during execution, clear guidance should be developed to enable rapid prosecution.

Liaison officers (LNO) from coalition partners, other components, and other Services are essential during dynamic targeting. LNOs—particularly the SOLE, BCD, and other government agencies (OGA)—may be able to provide the CFACC with additional options for dealing with emerging targets as well as provide locations and activities of friendly forces. LNOs work deconfliction issues and their forces on the ground can also assist friendly forces by finding, fixing, tracking, targeting, and assessing targets

Successful prosecution of a target during execution sometimes requires that targeting be completed in minutes. To achieve this time compression, the CFACC should consider implementing procedures that enable the phases of dynamic targeting to be performed simultaneously rather than sequentially. It has been common practice in the last several conflicts to establish a joint team dedicated to prosecution of TSTs. Dedicating teams to specific target categories may not always be advisable, however, since the entire COD is involved in the effort to prosecute dynamic targets and creating separate teams may result in unwanted isolation, impede unity of effort, and inhibit the cross-flow of information. Ideally, one joint COD team should perform targeting of all dynamic targets.

Successful prosecution of targets during execution also requires well organized and well rehearsed procedures for sharing sensor data and targeting information, identifying suitable strike assets, obtaining mission approval, and rapidly deconflicting weapon employment. The reaction time between the sensor and shooter can be greatly accelerated if there are clearly articulated objectives, guidance, priorities, and intent for dynamic targeting before targets are even identified. The appropriate response for each target depends heavily on the level of conflict, the clarity of the desired outcome, and ROE.

THE DYNAMIC TARGETING PORTION OF THE TASKING PROCESS

Dynamic targeting includes prosecution of several categories of targets:

✪ CFC-approved TSTs—targets of such high priority to friendly forces that the CFC designates them as requiring immediate response because they pose (or will soon pose) a danger to friendly forces or they are highly lucrative, fleeting targets of opportunity. The CFC is ultimately responsible for TST prosecution and relies upon the component commanders for conducting TST operations.

✪ Targets that are considered crucial for success of friendly component commanders' missions, but are not CFC-approved TSTs—for sake of convenience, these will be referred to in this chapter as "high payoff targets."

✪ Targets scheduled to be struck on the ATO being executed, but which have changed status in some way (such as FSCM changes).

✪ Other targets that emerge during execution that friendly commanders deem worthy of targeting, prosecution of which will not divert resources from higher-priority targets.

Each of the four categories of targets specified above is prosecuted via the same dynamic targeting portion of the tasking process—they differ only in relative priority.

CID plays an important part in dynamic targeting. For prospective targets, there are essentially three levels of CID that are relevant to CAOC personnel and those tasked to carry out actions against them. At the first level, the track or entity is identified as friendly, foe, or neutral. At the next level, the prospective target's type of platform is identified. This will aid in determining the nature of tactical action required against it and will assist in prioritizing the target. Finally, a third level entails determining the prospective target's intent (as by its track relative to friendly forces) when possible. This will further aid in establishing the prospective target's priority, and may sometimes entail reclassifying a target as a TST based on its potential threat to friendly forces.

Dynamic targeting consists of six distinct phases:

- ✪ Find.
- ✪ Fix.
- ✪ Track.
- ✪ Target.
- ✪ Engage.
- ✪ Assess.

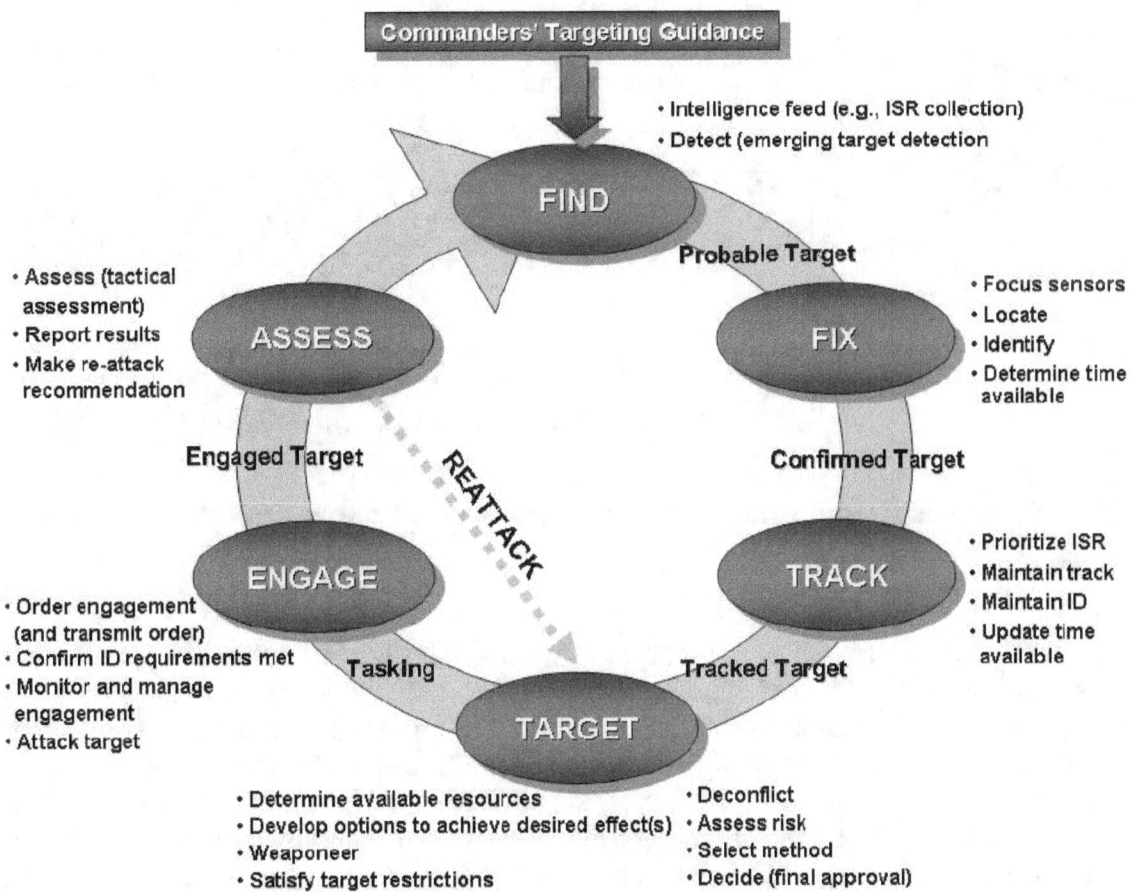

Figure 3.1. The Dynamic Targeting Process

The relationship of these phases to each other and the steps that compose them are illustrated in Figure 3.1. These are the same phases used to prosecute joint TSTs, as explained in the *Multi-Service Tactics, Techniques, and Procedures for Targeting Time-Sensitive Targets* (AFTTP(I) 3-2.3, also known as the "TST MTTP"). This method is commonly referred to as "F2T2EA" or colloquially as the "kill chain." Each of the phases is discussed below.

Find

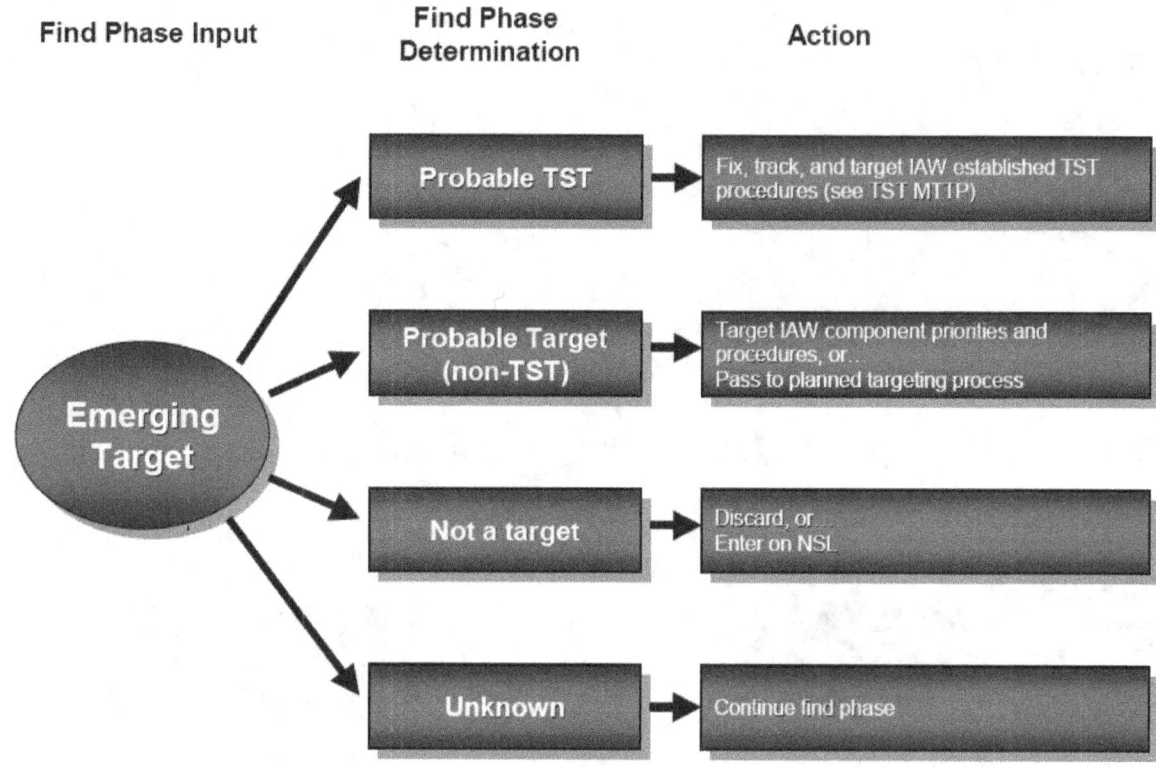

Find Phase Input   **Find Phase Determination**   **Action**

Emerging Target

Probable TST → Fix, track, and target IAW established TST procedures (see TST MTTP)

Probable Target (non-TST) → Target IAW component priorities and procedures, or... Pass to planned targeting process

Not a target → Discard, or... Enter on NSL

Unknown → Continue find phase

Figure 3.2. Find Phase Determinations and Follow-on Actions

The find phase involves ISR detection of an emerging target, some aspect of which suggests that it fits within one of the dynamic targeting categories listed above. The find phase requires clearly designated guidance from commanders, especially concerning target priorities, and the focused ISR collection plan based on IPB, to include named areas of interest and target areas of interest. Following this collection plan leads to detections, some of which will be "emerging targets"—detections that meet sufficient criteria (established by the CAOC with commander's guidance) to be considered and developed as a target. The time sensitivity and importance of this target may be initially undetermined. Emerging targets usually require further ISR and analysis to develop and confirm. This further analysis will result in one of four determinations which shape follow-on actions, as illustrated in Figure 3.2.

A good collection plan will not be passive. Commanders should not send out sensors without an idea of what they will collect. Instead, they should be anticipatory, which involves confirming anticipated results, not just blind detection. The result of the find phase is a probable target nominated for further investigation and development in the fix phase.

Fix

The fix phase positively identifies an emerging target as worthy of engagement and determines its position and other data with sufficient fidelity to permit engagement. It may begin when the emerging target is detected or after. When the emerging target is detected, sensors are focused on it to confirm its identity and precise location. This may require implementing a sensor network or diverting ISR assets from other uses to examine it. The CFACC may have to make the decision on whether diversion of ISR resources from the established collection plan is merited, but this decision can most often be made by COD personnel on the CAOC "ops floor." Data correlation and fusion confirms, identifies, and locates the target, resulting in its classification in one of the four target categories listed above. Target location and other information must be refined enough to permit engagement, which requires ISR capabilities that can identify stationary and mobile targets, day or night, in all weather, through all forms of terrain, camouflage, and concealment—all in a timely manner. Systems that can do this are a relatively recent development, and permit a degree of flexibility and timeliness that were not possible in the past. An estimation of the target's window of vulnerability frames the timeliness required for prosecution and may affect the prioritization of assets and risk assessment.

If a target is detected by the aircraft or system that will engage it (for example, by a missile-armed Predator, or a battle management command and control platform such as the airborne warning and control system [AWACS] or the joint surveillance target attack radar system [Joint STARS]), this may result in the find and fix phases being completed near-simultaneously, without the need for "traditional" ISR input. It may also result in the target and engage phases being completed without a lengthy coordination and approval process. Battle management systems can often fix target locations precisely enough to permit engagement without need for further ISR collection. Growth in sensor technology also permits "non-traditional" sources of ISR to supplement the find, fix, and track phases, integrating data from platforms other than those traditionally dedicated to intelligence collection to include information gleaned from weapons systems or even munitions themselves, helping to build a common operating picture that commanders can use to shorten the F2T2EA cycle.

Track

The track phase takes a confirmed target and its location, maintains a track on it, and confirms the desired effect against it. Sensors may be coordinated to maintain situational awareness (SA) or track continuity on targets. Windows of vulnerability should be updated when warranted. This phase requires relative reprioritization of ISR assets, just as the fix phase may, in order to maintain SA. If track continuity is lost, it will probably be necessary to reaccomplish the fix phase—and possibly the find phase as well. The track phase results in track continuity and maintenance of identification on the target, maintained by appropriate sensors or sensor combinations; a sensor prioritization scheme (if required); and updates on the target's window of vulnerability (if required). The process may also be run partially "in reverse" in cases where an emerging target is detected and engaged, but once it becomes clear it is a valid target, the sensors detecting it can examine recorded data to track the target back to its point of origin, such as a base camp, and thus potentially eliminate a wider threat or destroy more lucrative targets where only one might have been engaged without the benefit of newer tracking technologies. Such "point of origin hunting" has proven especially useful during stability and counterinsurgency operations such as those in Iraq.

Target

The target phase takes an identified, classified, located, and prioritized target; finalizes the desired effect and targeting solution against it; and obtains required approval to engage it. During this phase, COD personnel must review target restrictions, including collateral damage, ROE, LOAC, the NSL, the RTL, and FSCM. This phase accomplishes the equivalent of the "target validation" stage of the larger tasking cycle. It also accomplishes effects validation and weaponeering. COD personnel match available strike and sensor assets against desired effects, then formulate engagement options. They also submit assessment requirements.

The selection of assets for a specific target will be based on many factors, such as the location and operational status of ISR and strike assets, support asset availability, weather conditions, ROE, target range, the number and type of missions in progress, available fuel and munitions, the adversary threat, and the accuracy of targeting acquisition data. This can be the lengthiest phase due to the large number of requirements that must be satisfied. In many cases, however, dynamic targeting can be accelerated if target phase actions can be initiated and/or completed in parallel with other phases.

Engage

In this phase, identification of the target as hostile is confirmed and engagement is ordered and transmitted to the pilot, aircrew, or operator of the selected weapon system. The engagement orders must be sent to, received by, and understood by the "shooter." The engagement should be monitored and managed by the engaging component (for the air and space component, by the CAOC). The desired result of this phase is successful action against the target.

Assess

In this phase, predetermined assessment requests are measured against actions and desired effects on the target. ISR assets collect information about the engagement according to the collection plan (as modified during dynamic targeting) and attempt to determine whether desired effects and objectives were achieved. In cases of the most fleeting targets, quick assessment may be required in order to make expeditious re-attack recommendations. The subject of assessment is covered thoroughly in the next chapter.

OTHER CONSIDERATIONS

Engagement Authority

The authority to engage should be delegated to the C2 node that has the best information or situational awareness to execute the mission and direct communications to the operators and crews of the weapon systems involved. If the CFACC is delegated TST engagement authority by the CFC, that commander may delegate his engagement authority to a lower level (e.g., CAOC director or chief of combat operations). The CFACC has the authority to redirect those forces over which he has operational or tactical control. For all others, the affected component commander must approve all requests for redirection of apportioned air assets. Components execute the ATO as tasked and recommend changes to the CAOC as appropriate, given emerging CFC and component requirements.

At the tactical level, engagement authority normally resides with the "shooter" (aircrew, system operator, etc.) for those planned events on the current ATO being executed; this follows the tenet of decentralized execution. The fact that planned missions on an ATO have been approved for release by the CFACC passes engagement authority to the "shooters" personally executing those ATO missions, who must adhere to all guidance included in the ATO (SPINS, ACO, ROE, etc.). In dynamic targeting situations, where the target is not specified in the ATO prior to takeoff or execution, engagement may require that the "shooter" be "cleared to target" from a C2 entity outside the CAOC (like Joint STARS, AWACS, TACP, forward air controllers [ground or airborne]) due to identification or other criteria required prior to attack.

Engagement authority for those events that the CAOC maintains control over (like TSTs in many cases) will be passed to crews via tactical C2 means (AWACS, Joint STARS, etc.), with required criteria met when appropriate. Engagement authority for certain "sensitive" targets may reside at a higher level than the CFC, but will be passed appropriately through the component commander when the situation arises.

Placing the appropriate level of battlespace awareness at subordinate C2 nodes can streamline the C2 cycle and allow timely engagement during dynamic targeting. Decentralized C2 nodes should be able to exchange sensor, status, and target information with a fidelity that permits them to operate as a single, integrated C2 entity in order to effectively perform decentralized, coordinated execution of time-sensitive attacks.

Managing Increased Risk During Dynamic Targeting Operations

Understanding the level of acceptable risk is critical to successful targeting during execution. With compression of the decision cycle comes increased risk due to insufficient time for the more detailed coordination and deconfliction that takes place during deliberate targeting. Commanders must assess risk early, determine what constitutes acceptable risk, and communicate their intent. CFC guidance may stipulate acceptable risk when engaging TSTs. If it does not, then the CFACC must seek to obtain it. When new targets are acquired, Airmen in the CAOC and in the field must rely on commanders' guidance and their own experience to assess acceptable risk.

Particular targets may be determined to be such a threat to the force or to mission accomplishment that the CFACC is willing to accept a higher level of risk in order to attack the target immediately upon detection. Items to be considered in the risk assessment include:

✪ Risk to friendly forces (fratricide), risk to non-combatants, and collateral damage potential.

✪ LOAC and ROE compliance.

✪ Increased risk to attacking forces due to accelerated planning and coordination.

✪ Redundant attacks and wasting limited resources.

✪ Accepted use of non-optimal weapons and fuzing.

✪ Opportunity cost of diverting assets from their planned missions.

These considerations must be balanced against the danger of not attacking the target in time and thus risking mission failure, harm to friendly forces, or losing the opportunity to strike the target. More commonly, the risk associated with dynamic targeting involves the trade-off of diverting ISR and strike assets from already-scheduled missions to emerging targets. This should only be done when commanders' priority given to the new target exceeds that of the old. Proper planning (for such things as on-call assets) can mitigate much of this opportunity cost, however.

Handling Changes

The COD must be ready to respond with new targeting information in order to provide seamless operations when changes occur. These include things like:

✪ **Responding to changes in friendly operations**. For instance, if an aircraft tasked to prosecute a target has to abort for maintenance reasons, the COD must know the target's relative priority in order to provide appropriate targeting guidance. If the target is low priority, it may be best to place it on a subsequent day's ATO. If it is of higher priority, COD personnel will determine how best to direct or divert resources to prosecute it. COD personnel will have the best picture of what resources are available to prosecute it and what diverting resources may cost. Likewise, if an aircraft or package is diverted to prosecute a TST, the COD must identify the target(s) which will no longer be struck, as well as the new target which will be attacked. This information must be passed to the targeteers and collection managers to ensure coordinated collection and assessment on the new targets.

✪ **Responding to changes in weather**. A target planner's actions will be similar to when he responds to changes in friendly operations. Further, changes in weather may require changes to the platforms and/or weapons required to engage a particular target.

✪ **Re-targeting**. If a target that was to be prosecuted is no longer a viable target for whatever reason, targeteers must have alternate targets to assign to a strike mission. Time is important because assets may already be airborne

✪ **Responding to TSTs**. When a TST is identified, the COD must decide the best time to attack it. COD targeteers are involved in these efforts and provide guidance to planners concerning the characteristics and vulnerability of the target. Targeteers must be familiar with possible targets so that quick assessments and guidance can be given before the window of opportunity to strike the TST is gone.

Reduced Planning Time

Dynamic targeting has two significant limitations compared with deliberate targeting: the lack of detailed weaponeering and increased threat exposure. Commanders and the COD should consider these limitations when deciding whether to prosecute a target using dynamic targeting methods.

✪ **Weaponeering**. Due to the reduced planning time available, targets prosecuted using dynamic targeting will be engaged with less consideration given to key weaponeering issues such as fuze settings or axes of attack. In some cases, assets may be diverted to prosecute these targets with munitions not optimal for the given task. Since these considerations may carry increased risk of mission failure, collateral damage, or even harm to friendly troops, commanders must weigh the potential benefits gained by prosecuting the target quickly. Whenever possible, COD personnel should work with ISRD targeteers to ensure that proposed targeting solutions are sufficient for the given task. This often requires significant coordination.

✪ **Increased Threat**. High threat target areas are normally attacked by packages with dedicated support, such as electronic jamming and defense suppression munitions. The shortened dynamic targeting planning window may not allow for the same level of support, thereby exposing aircrews to greater risk. Time for target area threat analysis is also reduced, further increasing risk to the attacker.

Unit-Level Targeting Responsibilities

Individual flying units have targeting responsibilities that support and enhance CAOC efforts and tactical-level execution. Commanders, mission planners, and intelligence specialists within these units must ensure the validity and accuracy of the targeting information provided them for mission planning purposes. This responsibility may include verification of ATO guidance coordinates and adjudication of problems with the CAOC if errors or conflicts become evident. Specific data provided to mission planners should be checked for integrity, including verification of DPI coordinates and elevations, weapon azimuths and impact dive angles, and fuzing instructions when direct electronic transfer of such data is not possible or fails.

Considerable benefits can also be derived from air and ground units working together directly to accomplish mission planning at the tactical level when circumstances permit. Army ground liaison officers (GLOs) working with tactical air units can provide insight into ground component plans and offer direct coordination for missions flown in support of associated ground unit efforts. Such coordination can prove particularly useful during stability operations and other circumstances where air played primarily a supporting role, but can be beneficial during major combat operations as well, especially during urban operations or other similar situations requiring close coordination with ground units.

CHAPTER FOUR

ASSESSMENT

"...To fully exploit Air Force technological advances and operational capabilities, we must merge air, space, intelligence and information operations into a seamless capability. {We} must lead the way, linking the intelligence and information operations functions from the air and space domains to better support the decision maker."

—General Hal Hornburg,
Former Commander, Air Combat Command

GENERAL

Assessment encompasses all efforts to evaluate effects and gauge progress toward accomplishment of actions, effects, and objectives. It also helps evaluate requirements for future action. It helps answer two questions: "How is the conflict going?" and "what needs to be done next?" In an effects-based construct, it is not possible to think about actions and their effects without considering how accomplishment of those effects should be measured. Effects and objectives should always be measurable and planning for them should always include means of measurement and evaluation. Assessment is not really a separate "phase" of the air and space tasking—or any other—cycle, as descriptions and graphics often imply for the sake of conceptual clarity. Rather, it is interleaved throughout planning and execution and is integral to them. Its measures are determined during planning. It works together with planning to determine future courses of action. It is conducted in part during execution. It is an inseparable and integral component of the effects-based approach to conflict.

Over a decade of lessons learned from conflicts since DESERT STORM emphasize that the traditional concepts, practices, organizations, and tool sets constituting traditional "battle damage assessment" (BDA) do not meet warfighters' needs for assessment that can be acted upon in the high tempo of today's battlespace, or that encompasses the full spectrum of operations. The traditional approach to assessment is too focused on the tactical-level, requires CFC-level validation of all BDA (which significantly hampers management of federated assessment and slows the process), is more concerned with assessing actions than effects, and does not facilitate communication between federated partners. The very term BDA is limiting, since assessment extends well beyond "battle damage."

Any comprehensive view of assessment should tie evaluation of progress at the tactical level to all other levels of war, up to and including the national strategic level. The proper focus of assessment conducted by the air and space component should be on the operational level of war. An effective assessment construct should also support commanders' objectives at all levels, support commanders' decision cycles in real time, and provide the basis for analysis. To accomplish these things, an effective assessment construct must address the entire spectrum of operations and all levels of war, permit component validation of assessment elements, focus on effects, standardize federation, utilize intelligence specialties effectively, and integrate analysis efforts to the maximum extent possible.

MEASURES AND INDICATORS

At all levels of assessment, planners must choose criteria that describe or establish when actions have been accomplished, desired effects have been created, and objectives have been achieved. These criteria are called "measures and indicators." There are three distinct types of measures:

✪ **Measures of Performance**: Objective or quantitative measures assigned to the actions of a tactical task and against which a tactical task's accomplishment, in operations or missions terms, is assessed. MOP are associated with actions and thus exist only at the tactical level of conflict.

✪ **Measures of Effect**: Qualitative or quantitative measures assigned to an intended effect (direct or indirect), against which the effect's achievement is directly assessed. Some of these may be direct forms of measurement, like an eyewitness account of a bridge span being down; some may be more circumstantial indicators, such as measurements of traffic backed up behind a downed bridge.

✪ **Success Indicators (SI)**: The conditions indicating the progress toward or achievement of an objective or end-state condition. SI are normally qualitative and may be subjective. SI are normally developed from the most critical end state conditions that attainment of an objective will manifest in the operating environment. SI are independent from MOP and MOE and can exist at all levels of conflict, but primarily reside at the operational and strategic levels.

Measures and indicators are selected during planning. When selecting assessment measures, planners must identify the essential elements of information required to collect against them and provide guidance in the collection plan and JIPCL if special ISR or other PBA resources are needed. These measures must be refined or amended during the tasking cycle, as the tactical situation or the status of the target changes. Selection of assessment measures is an iterative, ongoing effort.

There may often be "gray areas" between MOP, MOE, and SI—empirical data supporting objective accomplishment, for instance—but all measures that determine accomplishment of objectives are SI, regardless of the level of war. **To be useful as a gauge of effectiveness, a measure,** whether an MOP, MOE, or SI, **must be meaningful, reliable, and either observable or capable of being reliably inferred**. Meaningful means it must be tied, explicitly and logically, to objectives at all levels. Reliable means it must accurately express the intended effect. If quantitative measures are used, they must be relevant. It is not sufficient to choose "fifty percent of enemy armor attrited" as an MOE without understanding *why* that measure is relevant to objectives. Observable means that existing intelligence collection methods can

GAUGING REGIME COLLAPSE

	STABLE REGIME				REGIME COLLAPSE
LEADERSHIP	Coherent Message Presence Governance Command & Control	Increased Rhetoric Few Leaders Visible Some Degraded Command & Control	Reliant on Lies Calls for Sacrifice	Calling for Citizens to Die for the Cause Leadership Disappearing Use of WMD	Regime Command, Control, & Communication Destroyed New Leaders Emerging
SECURITY APPARATUS	Stable Control Over Population Military Control Security Apparatus Functioning	Influence and Control Degraded	More Visible Control Attempts	Increase of Security Measures & Retribution	Fear & Power Base Destroyed
MILITARY	Volunteer / Special Forces Conscript / Regular Army	Regular Army Capitulating		Volunteer / Special Forces Resistance Collapsing	Armed Forces Not Resisting
POPULATION	Capital City Supportive Area Ambivalent Area	Uncertain Level of Support for US No Interference with US Actions	Accept US Actions Covert Support for US Actions	Civil Disobedience Overt Support for US Actions	Active Support of US Actions

Figure 4.1 Notional Example of Qualitative Assessment Measures

measure it.

Only MOE and SI are associated with OA and higher levels of assessment. They are qualitative, sometimes subjective measures, independent of MOP or other empirical measures that determine whether indirect effects and the objectives they lead to are being accomplished. Qualitative means primarily that judgment must be made in the absence of meaningful quantitative measures (see Figure 4.1 for a notional example). Military personnel tend to be less comfortable with these than with more empirical measures, since they are generally trained to regard their profession as more of a science than an art, but often the numbers themselves involved in quantitative measures can deceive. Seemingly "scientific" quantitative measures are often poorer representations of what should happen in the battlespace than more qualitative measures, like "enemy armor units A, B, and C not offering larger than platoon sized resistance to forces closing on Phase Line X until at least day Y." Such a measure may be much more relevant to the friendly scheme of maneuver, be easier to collect against, and be easier for commanders to act upon. It is often easier, especially at the higher levels of assessment, to choose qualitative measures that are logically tied to objectives. Quantitative measures, on the other hand, can, through their very seeming certainty, take on a life of their own, leading to actions that do not contribute to accomplishing objectives or the end state. For example, during DESERT STORM, strategic attack missions took down key nodes to deny power within the Iraqi electrical system. This effect was accomplished with little destruction of Iraqi civilian electrical power infrastructure. Nonetheless, many power generator plants were destroyed later in the campaign, in part because traditional empirical measurements of electrical capacity showed that the Iraqis still had substantial usable resources. This hampered civilian recovery following the campaign. This example also points out the importance of integrating assessment into employment planning and target development efforts early on.

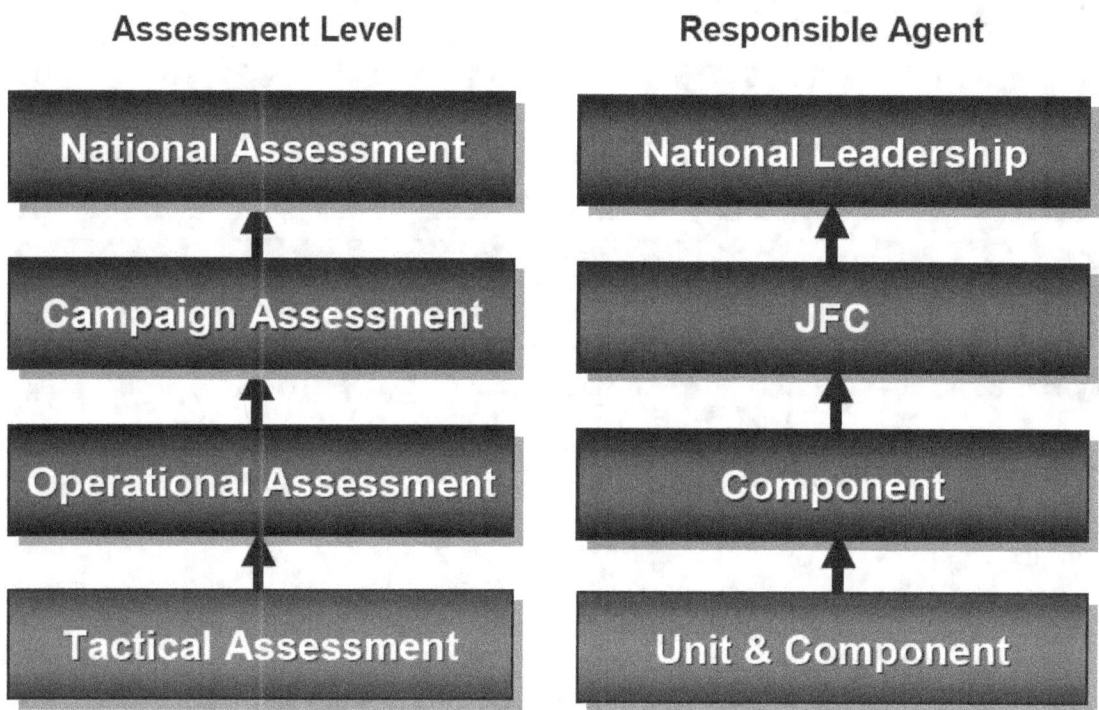

Figure 4.2. Four Levels of Assessment

THE FOUR LEVELS OF ASSESSMENT

Assessment consists of four distinct but interrelated levels:

○ **Tactical Assessment**: Determination of the effectiveness of kinetic and non-kinetic tactical military operations through empirical and objective methods

- **Operational Assessment**: Evaluation of effects generated by tactical actions and other battlespace influences toward achieving component operational objectives and recommendations for future action

- **Campaign Assessment**: The CFC's broad qualitative and analytical determination of the overall effectiveness of military operations and recommendations for future action

- **National Assessment**: Broad review of the effectiveness of national security strategy and whether national leadership's objectives for a particular crisis or contingency are being met

Tactical Assessment (TA)

Tactical Assessment is the evaluation of tactical actions against assigned tactical tasks. "Performance-based" means that it uses empirical, objective, usually quantifiable measures when collecting and analyzing data from tactical actions. TA assessors take this collected data; aggregate, analyze, and archive it; and determine details commanders will need in order to take further action. In many cases, TA assessors may make a recommendation for re-attack, especially if it is clear that a scheduled action was not successful. TA answers such questions as:

- Was the intended action accomplished?

- Was the intended direct effect accomplished?

- Has the target's status changed?

- Is re-engagement, re-attack, or "re-influence" necessary?

TA feeds higher levels of effects-based assessment. In the current era of low-level global conflict punctuated by frequent large campaigns, it is also imperative that TA, like all levels of assessment, be able to analyze and perform meaningful evaluations across the entire spectrum of military conflict.

TA consists of several component elements:

- **Physical damage assessment (PDA)** estimates the extent of physical damage to a target based upon observation or empirically based interpretation. PDA involves cooperative effort between units in the field and the CAOC. Sometimes it utilizes data from other components or national agencies. Sources such as inflight reports (INFLTREP), MISREP, and weapon system video are commonly used to generate PDA.

- **Functional assessment (FA)** estimates the remaining functional or operational capability of a targeted object or entity. FA is usually inferred from reported physical damage and should include estimates of recuperation or replacement time. Note, however, that targets affected by many IO and other non-kinetic capabilities will often not have physical damage, requiring assessors to perform FA in the absence of PDA. Assessment planners must anticipate appropriate measures and indicators for such effects.

✪ **Munitions effectiveness assessment (MEA)** evaluates whether the selected weapon or munition functioned as intended. It examines the munitions' known parameters, the delivery tactics used, and the interaction between the munition and the delivery platform. MEA is fed back into the planning process to validate or adjust weaponeering and platform selections. It is also the form of assessment with the highest potential "payoff" in terms of weapons and tactics development, because the data it generates is fed into the JMEM revision process, resulting in more accurate future weaponeering.

✪ **Estimated damage analysis (EDA)**: Many times during execution, it is not possible to wait on ISR verification of strike results without inordinately delaying higher-level assessments. EDA is the technique of using existing munitions effectiveness or other data to estimate weapons effectiveness on targets. This information is used to determine if collection assets other than those inherent in the weapon(s), aircraft, or aircrew are required to establish the level of physical and functional damage inflicted on selected targets. EDA focuses on estimations of weapons effectiveness and therefore allows the commander to accept risk in the absence of other information, and is appropriate for all but high-priority targets.

✪ **Lower-scale conflict assessment** is an evolving area of assessment and is comparatively recent. In smaller-scale contingencies and stability operations, there may be significant play of non-military instruments of national power and considerable interaction between the military and non-DOD or nongovernmental agencies. These may require assessment at the tactical level that is required for higher effects-based operational- and strategic-level assessments. Exactly what form these assessments will take at the tactical level is hard to say, but will be tied to demands that are specific to the conflict and the cultures or nations it is waged in. In smaller conflicts, the degree of interest from command echelons above component level may be greater, as may the need for timeliness in tactical and higher-level assessments. These operations will require analytical skills ranging far beyond weapons effects into political, socio-economic, cultural-ideological, psychological and international arenas. It will also require coordination with analytical and academic centers outside the DOD.

✪ **Weather and environmental effects** can play a considerable role in determining the results of targeting actions. At the tactical level, combat weather flights (CWF) are responsible for determining and integrating weather effects into the decision cycle. At the component level, weather personnel assigned to the CAOC assess and integrate weather effects into near-term execution decisions, as well as longer-term strategy considerations. Additionally, operational weather squadrons help anticipate weather effects by providing CWFs and other weather personnel with accurate common characterizations of the current and future environment.

✪ **Logistics status**: Tactical action results in the expenditure of munitions, fuel, and other materiel. This must be tracked and shown to commanders as part of a comprehensive view of current and projected friendly capability.

Units in the field perform some of the TA functions, but "ownership" of TA should be at the functional (or Service) component level. Incorporating all the elements listed above into an amalgamated TA effort owned by component commanders will greatly expedite TA and will thus make timely and relevant higher-level, effects-based assessment possible. Within the CAOC, several divisions share responsibility for TA. The ISRD develops PDA, with inputs from the COD and units. They must rapidly evaluate MISREPs, weapon system video, and other available intelligence to recommend immediate restrike to the COD or to commanders. EDA is accomplished by targeteers in the ISRD and CPD. Those same targeteers are critical team members in the MEA process, providing inputs as part of a collective responsibility with operations experts. While some FA may be accomplished at the CAOC level, most is performed by the theater joint intelligence operations center (JIOC) or through reachback or federated support (see Chapter Five), due to demands for expertise, resources, manning, and the battle rhythm. Weather effects are determined by the WST, leveraging reachback support from the operational weather unit for their region. Logistics inputs may come from many sources, including the COMAFFOR's A-4 (Logistics) and the AMD. Lower-intensity conflict types of MOPs may have to come from interagency federated support or even from sources outside US control. Assessment of non-kinetic action and non-lethal effects may require significant coordination with the SD's OAT and the CAOC's IO Flight.

Operational Assessment (OA)

Operational assessment at the component level is the first truly effects-based echelon of assessment. TA includes evaluation of direct effects and some immediate indirect, second-order effects, but OA is the first level at which complex, indirect effects are evaluated, progress toward objectives is measured, and recommendations for future action extending beyond simple physical re-attack are made. In one sense, TA is "historical" or "confirmatory"—it tells what has happened, as an aid to determining whether friendly forces are "doing things right." OA is a crucial form of assessment that should be more "anticipatory" or "predictive," seeking to answer whether friendly forces are "doing the right thing." The focus of OA is also much broader than TA's, expanding from simple destruction, attrition, or damage to the entire range of effects options. OA answers mid- to long-term (days and beyond) questions such as:

✪ Are component objectives being achieved? If not, why not?

✪ Does friendly level of effort need to be modified for this phase of the operation?

✪ Does component strategy need to be adjusted? If so, how?

✪ Are there unanticipated operational limitations?

✪ Do objectives need to be modified? If so, how?

OA builds upon TA, incorporating other elements as well:

Aggregate of TA products: Includes all the results of TA relevant to particular effects and objectives. However, OA may not be able to wait on a complete TA picture before delivering "actionable" advice to commanders. OA measures are qualitative, and while they build upon what objective data is available, they sometimes entail informed but subjective judgment concerning accomplishment of effects.

Several key elements of PBA feed OA:

✪ **Target system assessment**: An estimate of the overall effectiveness of force employment against selected enemy target systems. This is a component-level fusion of FA products against targets in a particular system, using them to assess overall impact upon a system's capabilities. It is particularly important that this assessment be based on desired effects rather than simple empirical measures of damage. Many times, effects against systems like electricity and communications can be achieved with little physical damage.

✪ **Evaluation of enemy action and intent** is a critical prerequisite to evaluation of progress toward objectives. Some of this assessment can be empirical: disposition of enemy units, amount of enemy electronic or aerial activity, and so on. Much, of necessity, will entail qualitative evaluation, especially as assessors tackle the problem of enemy intent. This part of OA will likely be accomplished in tandem with the equivalent portions of CFC-level campaign analysis and with federated and reachback support.

Risk assessment considers the risks of friendly attrition, political cost from collateral damage and other unintended indirect effects, the cost of lost opportunities involved in pursuing the chosen COA, and the consequences of failure to achieve the objective(s) to develop a comprehensive picture of the potential costs of friendly action. This is a vital input to evaluation of progress and recommendations for future action.

The full range of military operations—stability, engagement, deterrence, and other aspects of smaller-scale contingencies—are more important here than in TA. In smaller conflicts, it may be necessary to consider "strategic" issues, such as how effectively other instruments of national power (like diplomatic, informational, and economic) are integrated with military efforts. This may also require evaluation of coalition efforts. The largest share of responsibility for this form of assessment normally rests with the CFC, but some may be relevant to the component level and component assessment inputs will be usually be required to accomplish campaign assessment.

Evaluation of progress toward objectives is one of the two most important elements of OA. This is fundamentally an effects-based and qualitative evaluation, building upon empirical data, but involving significant analyst and commander judgment. Sometimes there will be very little objective data pointing toward accomplishment. As discussed in the sections on effects, many indirect effects are hard to measure until they happen. Planners and commanders must be patient and counsel patience in light of this—success may be around the corner, even if this is hard to see predictively.

Recommending future action is the other vitally important aspect of OA. Based on analysis of the other elements, OA recommends continuing, modifying, or completely changing the component strategy. Resulting recommendations may include such things as shifting the priority of air and space targeting, changing the overall weight of effort, transitioning to another operational phase, or branch initiation.

OA is primarily a component responsibility. Again, in the more traditional assessment construct, operational assessment was solely the province of the CFC and his staff, but this does not represent best practice, any more than it does for TA. Within the CAOC, OA is the responsibility of the SD operational assessment team, using resources and personnel from the ISRD to collect and collate needed information. OA will also likely involve component coordination directly with reachback and federated partners. There is still a large of piece of assessment that must reside at the CFC's level. This is called campaign assessment.

The problem with getting into an accounting numbers game is the number of things, whether they're SAM radars,...MiG-21s, or SU-17s, the numbers are normally inaccurate. The going-in position [is] the intel community will work with us on how many they could possibly have or how many they purchased or how many they had X number of weeks ago or months ago. What you don't know is how many are operable.

—General T. Michael "Buzz" Moseley
Chief of Staff of the Air Force (CSAF); at the time OIF CFACC
Press interview, 5 April 2003

Campaign Assessment (CA)

Campaign assessment is essentially OA accomplished at the CFC's level. Its focus is broader, however, since the CFC must consider how all components' actions contribute to overall accomplishment of campaign objectives. CA must also consider how other instruments of national power are being integrated with military efforts, regardless of the scale of the conflict, and must evaluate coalition efforts as well. CA answers long-term questions like,

- Are overall campaign objectives being achieved? If not, why not?
- Does the campaign strategy need to be adjusted? If so, how?
- Should the campaign transition to a new phase, branch, or sequel?
- How are operations impacting follow-on or end state considerations?

CA consists of the same elements as OA, but is an amalgamation of component operational, rather than tactical, assessments. CA is accomplished by the CFC's staff, principally the J-2, with extensive federated support. The CAOC provides inputs to CA through its OA products and receives CA products that can be used by the CFACC and the SD to modify air and space component strategy through the AOD. The SD and ISRD must thus have extensive and frequent interaction with the CFC's J-2. These relationships are best cemented in peacetime, but this is not always possible in an age of expeditionary operations. At very least, CAOC assessors should seek to build these relationships during planning, just as they must with federated partners.

National Assessment (NA)

National assessment takes the accumulated results of CA from around the world and combines it with assessments of the effectiveness of other instruments of national power to build an evaluation of how strategic objectives are being met in a particular conflict and how progress in various conflicts is contributing to achievement of national security objectives. There is no single formal process for this type of assessment at present. It is accomplished by many agencies in many departments of the executive branch of the government, such as the Office of the Secretary of Defense and the President's National Security Council. Detailed treatment of this level of assessment is beyond the scope of this document, but products of it may often influence the conduct of campaigns and operations.

THE ASSESSMENT PROCESS

Regardless of the level of conflict, everyone involved in the targeting process should incorporate a means for conducting assessment of their mission. **Regardless of the level of assessment, the process of analyzing the adversary, choosing appropriate measures, evaluating progress, and recommending action consists of the same four basic steps: Define, monitor, analyze, and recommend.** These are discussed below.

Define. Operational objectives, tactical objectives, and tactical tasks, along with the associated MOE and MOP, are defined during JAOP development. The supporting metrics provide indicators used during TA and OA. Having well-defined assessment criteria in the JAOP provides the entire CAOC with a clear indication of what the CFACC intends to accomplish for the CFC. The job of those tasked with assessment responsibility then becomes one of examining how well the CFACC is using air, space and information capabilities to achieve objectives. JAOP-derived measures should be refined into tactical-level requirements and measures during the planning portions of the tasking cycle.

Monitor. Monitoring the situation will likely be the most time- and resource-intensive aspect of assessment. The CAOC must monitor both the friendly and enemy situation. They must monitor combat operations and all the other factors that may have an impact on the situation. The act of monitoring does not serve each level of assessment discretely, but serves all forms of assessment simultaneously, even though certain ISR platforms are collecting against specific requirements. Monitoring requires extensive expertise from a wide variety of sources: intelligence, operations, other components' liaisons, federated and reachback partners, and so on.

Analyze. Assessors must take a critical look at the supporting metrics defining success in achieving tasks and objectives to provide commanders with a coherent picture drawn from an often-overwhelming stream of data. The data are not directly useful to commanders in most cases. Intelligence, targeting, and strategy personnel must evaluate the data stream and glean what is useful and significant from it. This is the most conceptually difficult part of the process, even if it consumes fewer man-hours than monitoring, but is essential if commanders are to have assessment products they can act upon. Even TA entails analysis, as there is sometimes considerable "art" to determining even physical damage levels based on sensor data.

Recommend. Recommendations may range from a simple, near-immediate re-attack call from the COD to advising a major change in campaign strategy, depending upon the level of assessment involved. They may include such things as shifting of air operations priority, weight of effort, and branch or sequel initiation. Even at the operational level, they may include lesser measures such as modifying the MOE to reflect new requirements, or utilizing new capabilities or forces.

Metrics

The SD should develop metrics to determine if air operations are properly linked to the overall air and space strategy and the larger hierarchy of campaign and national objectives. These metrics evaluate the results achieved during air and space operations. Metrics can either be objective (using sensors or aircrews to directly observe damage inflicted) or subjective (using indirect means to ascertain results) depending on the metric applied to either the objective or task. Both qualitative and quantitative metrics should be used to avoid unsound or distorted results. Metrics can either be inductive (using sensors or personnel to directly observe the battlespace and build SA cumulatively) or deductive (using indirect means to deduce results from what was previously known of the adversary and battlespace). Measures of success are indications that the effects achieved are influencing enemy activity in desired ways among various target systems.

I'll tell you up front that our sensors show that the preponderance of the Republican Guard divisions that were outside of Baghdad are now dead. We've laid on these people. I find it interesting when folks say we're softening them up. We're not softening them up, we're killing them.

**—General T. Michael "Buzz" Moseley
CSAF; at the time OIF CFACC
Press interview, 5 April 2003**

Tactical tasks identify the focus areas for application of air and space power in support of tactical objectives. MOP evaluate the immediate activity performed to assess tactical tasks. Paired with the tasks, MOP use performance assessment techniques to determine "if we're doing things right" to achieve success. MOP lend themselves to quantitative and/or statistical analysis techniques, based on reported observations and facts. Assessors should craft MOP that are meaningfully objective (quantitative), understandable, relevant, collectable, and logically tied to the hierarchy of effects and objectives.

Key Enablers

Implementing a more comprehensive view of assessment will enhance situational awareness, make "actionable" assessment easier, and facilitate commanders' decision-making. Several issues should be addressed in order to enable and enhance this process.

Accurate ATO Tracking. Accurate tracking and reporting of ATO results is essential for effective TA, the first vital link in the assessment chain. Implementing innovations like using an ATO coordinator ("football carrier") to process a given ATO through its entire life cycle, and instituting a combat reports cell within the COD may facilitate this.

Air Force Reachback and Joint / National Federation. Develop relationships and agreements by which components can work directly with reachback and federated partners as necessary. For example, if analysts at DIA are helping determine the capability of the adversary's integrated air defense system (IADS), CAOC targeteers and assessors should be allowed to work directly with DIA action officers to obtain the best means of implementing desired effects like air dominance. Insisting that the DIA may only work directly with the joint force intelligence directorate (J-2), as is often now done, adds an unnecessary layer of bureaucracy that extends planning and assessment timelines.

Integrated C2 Systems. Targeting systems and databases should be able to interface with collection management systems and databases, which should in turn interface seamlessly with the theater battle management core system (TBMCS), and so on up the chain.

Automation. Computers are making it possible to automate much of the manual labor required in targeting and assessment, freeing CAOC personnel from being database and target list managers and allowing them to concentrate on targeting and planning issues.

CHAPTER FIVE

READINESS AND ONGOING RESPONSIBILITIES FOR TARGETING

 *...our product in war is dead targets, and our product in peace is all that goes into generating the warrior proficiency that kills those targets in wartime.*

—General John P. Jumper
Former CSAF
24 February 2000

GENERAL

Targeting does not begin and end within the air tasking cycle. It neither starts when a conflict starts, nor ends when a conflict ends. Targeting is a 24/7, 365 days-a-year effort. This chapter refers to those activities that should be accomplished prior to the onset of hostilities as "targeting readiness."

According to the Unified Command Plan, each geographic or functional combatant commander is assigned a COMAFFOR. Targeting readiness is the responsibility of the COMAFFOR.

Each COMAFFOR has certain targeting resources (principally personnel) assigned to him to conduct required targeting activities. In practice, however, targeting is federated among many different units and organizations. It is the COMAFFOR's responsibility to ensure these various organizations are conducting their duties so as to meet the needs of specific deliberate, crisis action, and campaign planning efforts, to include OPLAN, contingency plan (CONPLAN), and JAOP development. This is often easier said than done, as many of these agencies do not fall under the COMAFFOR's control and likely have competing priorities. For instance, Air Combat Command's 480th Intelligence Wing, headquartered at Langley AFB, which provides operational

✪ **Target Development**
✪ **Point Mensuration**
✪ **Weaponeering**
✪ **Assessment**
✪ **BE Number & DPI Standardization**
✪ **Database Management**
✪ **Datum Management**
✪ **Establishing CAOC Relationships**
✪ **Establishing Federated and Reachback Relationships**
✪ **Equipping Targeting Organizations**
✪ **Training and Exercises**

**Figure 5.1.
Readiness Responsibilities
for Targeting**

intelligence to combatant commanders, consists of several physically separated squadrons and does not fall under any geographic combatant command. As such, it is called upon to support US Air Forces Europe (USAFE), Central Air Forces (CENTAF), Pacific Air Forces (PACAF), and other targeting efforts, often at the same time. Unless clear guidance or memoranda of agreement are put in place, a COMAFFOR may see part of his expected federated targeting infrastructure assigned to other tasks. Effective delineation of duties is critical if this federated targeting system is to work in both peace and war. Such federated support is necessary for all aspects of ongoing targeting readiness, and is important to keep in mind while addressing specific targeting duties.

Targeting duties are typically the responsibility of the targeteers in air intelligence squadrons (AIS) and information operations teams (IOT). These units provide the core personnel for an air intelligence group (AIG) or air and space operations group (AOG), depending on the theater. Commanders of these units must ensure that their personnel are conducting all necessary targeting planning activities for their areas of responsibility during peacetime.

TARGET DEVELOPMENT

Much of peacetime targeting readiness is geared toward target development. Targeteers work closely with AIS intelligence analysts to develop target intelligence and target system models. However, they may have to coordinate with many types of intelligence analysts (general military intelligence, imagery, signals intelligence [SIGINT], human intelligence [HUMINT], etc.), outside of the CAOC. See Appendix B for specifics. Even if there are no official federation procedures in place, CAOC targeteers should still work with these organizations to utilize their expertise.

PRISTINA MILITARY POLICE, SERBIA

Selection of targets is dependent on a systematic study of available intelligence. Without such intelligence and its systematic analysis there can be no rational planning for the application of air power. An organization with a high degree of analytical competence is required to perform this targeting function. It requires competent, trained personnel who understand the capabilities and limitations of intelligence as well as aerospace [sic] forces. These individuals must have access to a current database and the knowledge to use it. Finally, as the [United States Strategic Bombing Survey] states, the lack of this ability at the beginning of a future national emergency might prove disastrous!

—John Glock
"The Evolution of Air Force Targeting," Airpower Journal, Fall 1994

Ideally, target development should support an OPLAN or CONPLAN, which provides required targeting guidance and forms the basis for a JAOP that can be used in actual conflict. In reality, the US often enters contingencies without established deliberate planning products, or those that exist require extensive modification when an actual contingency arises. Obviously, it is impossible to have a plan for every conceivable contingency, but waiting to conduct target development until a contingency develops will put planners at a huge disadvantage. Targeteers must utilize existing IPB products to identify areas and subjects that may be of concern in the future. Even without established plans to guide them, targeteers should always seek out as much guidance from commanders as they can. Target development should always be geared toward achieving certain valid objectives, and all effects and actions that targeteers recommend should support those objectives. In some targeting methodologies, such as TSA discussed in Chapter Two, targeteers derive notional objectives based on tasks their theater is likely to receive and they base their target development on these objectives. Such a technique can be used even where formal TSA methodologies are not implemented.

Target Folders

Target development results in the creation of a target folder (either electronic or physical) which includes the justification for considering the entity a target and detailed information on the target to guide further planning efforts. Each target should have a single target folder. Because theater JIOC and other Services have targeteers supporting deliberate and contingency planning efforts, it is important for AIS targeteers to coordinate with these organizations to avoid duplication of effort when building target folders. This is especially important when clear planning guidance is lacking or a delineation of duties among the Service and functional commands has not yet been properly established.

Joint Target List

Once targeteers have adequately developed targets and target systems to determine the causal linkages that help to achieve specific effects and objectives, they must nominate them for inclusion in the appropriate JTL for a specific plan or contingency. Normally the combatant command's J-2 maintains this list. Communication between AIS targeteers and the J-2 is critical to ensure effective prosecution of specific targets once hostilities begin. Methods of nomination vary with each theater. In the event J-2 is not maintaining the JTLs for whatever reason, the AIS or AOG should maintain the lists itself, in accordance with any applicable combatant command directives.

No-Strike and Restricted Target Lists

During targeting efforts, targeteers nominate targets for inclusion on NSLs and RTLs. Like JTLs, these lists are usually maintained by the J-2. See Chapter Two for details. Building them in peacetime will help reduce the possibility of attacking entities that are protected from attack (based on ROE, LOAC, or international law) and help speed target development once the battle rhythm has started.

Collateral Damage Estimates

Often, a target is on the RTL or NSL because of CD concerns. Thus, CD analysis begins during peacetime target development. Historically, individual theaters conducted CD estimation according to their own standards. Chairman of the Joint Chiefs of Staff directives now provide a coherent five-level process that standardizes DOD CD practices. Although some aspects of estimating CD occur during weaponeering, targeteers, in conjunction with intelligence analysts, can begin the process by applying general CD rules for identifying buildings, structures, areas, or other entities in proximity to an intended target that may be of concern. As non-kinetic and non-lethal weapons proliferate, CD concerns may go beyond typical kinetic effects. Information operations specialists can assist in identifying such non-kinetic CD concerns.

PBA begins on D minus 365

—General John P. Jumper,
Former CSAF
Remarks to the 2002 Air and Space Conference,
Washington D.C., 7 Mar 2002

Intelligence Gaps

Often, lack of adequate intelligence may hinder comprehensive target development. In such cases, targeteers should identify intelligence gaps and submit requests for intelligence collection, analysis, and/or production that will give them the information they need to complete target development. All production requests are given to the AIS ISR operations flight for submission. This is true for planners assigned to both the AIS as well as those assigned to other flights or squadrons in the AIG or AOG.

POINT MENSURATION

Mensuration is simply the act of precisely measuring something. It is commonly used in targeting parlance to refer to the exact measurement of a target's geographical coordinates. Point mensuration has always been an important part of targeting, since the points measured represent the DPIs for the munitions employed. As the accuracy of weapons delivery has improved, the importance of mensuration has grown in proportion. Accurate mensuration is a vital part of today's targeting. Due to the potential consequences of inaccurately mensurating coordinates, the Joint Chiefs of Staff have mandated that those involved in point mensuration be certified to do it according to Joint Chiefs of Staff instructions. When accomplished before ATO execution, it permits employment of an entire class of weapons (those, like global positioning system (GPS)-aided and cruise missiles that guide to pre-set coordinates).

This also allows CAOC personnel to significantly shorten the dynamic targeting "kill chain." GPS-aided weapons are not so much "smart" as they are "obedient." They guide to the mensurated point they are programmed to attack, so accurate mensuration is vital to their employment. Mensuration is not required for accurate employment of all weapons, however.

Because mensuration is a form of measurement, errors are inevitable and the extent of the estimated error must be captured as part of the coordinate. The standard method endorsed by National Geospatial-Intelligence Agency (NGA) is to express coordinate accuracy as a "circular error" (CE) and vertical accuracy as a "linear error" (LE) to a 90 percent degree of certainty (CE/LE 90%). When NGA validates a mensuration software algorithm, it is actually the fidelity of the CE/LE accuracy estimates over a range of mensuration situations that is judged. These estimates are used during weaponeering to derive type and quantity of weapons, and targeting coordinate data must be considered incomplete without them. The modernized intelligence database and the ATO both have coordinate accuracy fields for this reason.

The effort to mensurate coordinates, especially for a target set with a large number of DPIs, can be extremely long. Technological advances have helped shorten the effort somewhat, but for the time being at least, it will remain manpower- and time-intensive. If this planning is not conducted beforehand, it may adversely affect the CAOC's battle rhythm or even unit mission planning. Conversely, targeteers may become rushed, leading to mensuration errors that prevent effective employment or have unwanted effects like CD. Targeteers will not know what munitions will be used to prosecute a target, thus the more precise they are in mensurating coordinates, the more options they will give targeteers during a conflict. Again, this effect is magnified during dynamic targeting.

WEAPONEERING

Like point mensuration, weaponeering can be very time-consuming. Thus, the more that is accomplished prior to hostilities, the more options planners will have during a conflict. For example, if a targeteer only weaponeers for GBU-12s against a certain DPI prior to hostilities, then GBU-12s are the only option to prosecute the DPI during combat unless there is sufficient time to weaponeer another munition. This has ripple effects, since it entails reevaluation of such things as CD criteria. Even if there is time, this will slow weaponeering of other targets and may even affect the battle rhythm. The more done prior to conflict, the more weaponeering options commanders and planners have during conflict.

Weaponeering will not diminish in importance because of non-kinetic and non-lethal weapons. Rather, it will increase the importance of pre-conflict weaponeering. Providing commanders and planners with options prior to hostilities, rather than developing options during hostilities, gives them more time to consider the best course of action. Anticipation is the best way to compress the decision cycle.

ASSESSMENT

In the "traditional" view of assessment, there is little to do outside of ongoing operations. This is untrue. Personnel involved in assessment can review pre-conflict target development materials and try to determine appropriate MOE for them. In fact, this should go hand-in-hand with peacetime target development, just as it should during conflict. Assessment personnel should also cultivate relationships with federated partners during peacetime, to expedite flow of information once conflict begins. Finally, information and other non-kinetic weapons, as well as the low-intensity transnational nature of the Global War on Terror, have made the possibility of less overt force employment a reality. Things may be happening in many parts of the world that require astute and thorough assessment, even if major campaigns are not being conducted.

The traditional approach to assessment has led to underutilization of "assessors" in peacetime. Often, there is little emphasis on their specialty until a commander asks, "How are we doing?" during operations. Commanders should ensure assessors are properly utilized in peacetime by encouraging them to foster the necessary federated relationships and by encouraging them to study targeting and assessment from prior operations to determine how a conflict in their theater would be affected. Every conflict is different, but many concepts hold true regardless of where the conflicts are fought. For example, adversaries may use the same aircraft and munitions regardless of theater. Many nations have similar weaponry, even if how they use them differs. Also, as CAOCs become more standardized, the opportunity to learn lessons from other CAOCs increases. For instance, assessors may learn from a conflict like OIF about the difficulties associated with accurately assessing how a nation's C2 network is functioning once it has been attacked and can take steps to minimize this in their theater.

Peacetime commanders can further assist wartime performance of their assessment personnel by protecting them from excessive non-assessment taskings and by ensuring adequate manning of assessment cells. These cells should include personnel from operations, intelligence, IO, and space specialties at a minimum.

Another important aspect of assessment during peacetime is the role MEA plays in helping guide munitions procurement. The specifics of this subject are outside the scope of this publication, but one of the main purposes of MEA is to guide the process of weapon acquisition and modification and to feed JMEM revision in order to produce better weapons and weaponeering solutions.

BASIC ENCYCLOPEDIA NUMBER (BE#) AND DPI STANDARDIZATION

All targeteers in the CAOC should understand the theater BE# plan for a conflict. While many targets already have BE#s assigned, many identified during combat do not have them. Without an established plan for assigning BE#s, components may take it upon themselves to assign them, creating the potential for confusion and lack of situational awareness on what targets are being struck. Confusion can adversely affect the battle rhythm or, worse, result in targeting errors. Thus, CAOC targeteers should coordinate with their combatant command's J-2 to ensure a standardized BE# naming convention is used. Standard DPI numbering is also important, and the joint targeting committee is finalizing the adoption of the joint designated point of impact (JDPI) concept using a six-character format with a central numbering registry involving the joint commands and allied nations. A theater DPI registry will ensure standardization of DPIs and eliminate duplication and possible error.

The convention should address both static and mobile targets. It is usually not feasible to assign standard BE#s to mobile targets. However, for proper data base management, such mobile targets still require some sort of identification. While the numbers may not be actual BE#s, the theater must still have some way of identifying the target. Again, CAOC planners should understand the theater naming convention to minimize targeting errors and the time needed for effective air planning.

DATABASE MANAGEMENT

Proper database management is necessary for effective targeting. Many systems used in the field are "stovepiped" and cannot talk to one another. If interoperable systems and databases are not available, it is the targeteer's responsibility to develop procedures (in peacetime) to overcome the difficulties associated with using systems that are not interoperable. There are many users of information in the CAOC. Ideally, everyone should work from the same database, but this is rarely the case.

Targeteers must coordinate with many different teams to ensure the flow of information in the CAOC is as seamless as possible. Those with whom targeteers should coordinate include (but are not limited to):

✪ **Analysis, Correlation, and Fusion Team** (ACFT). The ACFT in the ISRD is responsible for updating enemy order of battle (EOB) databases. Targeteers must be able to pull from this database to ensure targeteers are using the most current EOB.

✪ **ISR Operations Team**. The ISR operations team in the ISRD is responsible for planning and coordinating intelligence-gathering missions by CFACC assets. They also have insight into intelligence-gathering platforms the CFACC does not own, including spacecraft. Ensuring targeting and collection management databases are the same will cut down the time required to task collection assets to support targeting efforts, especially in the case of dynamic targeting.

✪ **Tactical Assessment Cell**. The TA cell in the ISRD is responsible for assessing the immediate results and effects of tactical operations. Often, these assessments lead to some type of follow-on action by friendly forces.

✪ **Combat Operations Intelligence Team**. The ISR Team in the COD, led by (and sometimes consisting only of) the senior intelligence duty officer (SIDO), provides intelligence support to ATO execution in the areas of analysis, collection management, targeting, and assessment. Having main targeting databases interact with those in combat operations is essential for seamless targeting support when the ATO requires modification. This importance is magnified when supporting dynamic targeting operations, especially those involving TSTs.

⊕ **Dynamic Targeting Team**. The targeting team in the COD works for the dynamic targeting team chief, but closely coordinates with the SIDO's personnel. This team consists of, at a minimum, a target intelligence duty officer and a target duty technician.

⊕ **Operational Assessment Team**. The OAT in the SD is responsible for determining whether or not desired effects are being created and if those effects are leading to the attainment of CFACC and CFC objectives. The targeting database must match up with that used by the OAT so that specific targets can be tracked to specific effects and objectives.

⊕ **Strategy Plans Team**. The strategy plans team in the SD is responsible for building the overall CFACC strategy and is responsible for producing the JAOP. This phase of planning may involve a need to access targeting databases in order to support JAOP creation.

⊕ **Information Operations Team**. The IOT is responsible for identifying opportunities to achieve desired effects primarily through non-kinetic means. Based upon its full integration throughout the CAOC planning cycle, the IOT is also often able to recommend different options or parallel courses of action to maximize success in achieving a specific effect.

...the critical linchpin for both the error in identification of the building and the failure of the review mechanisms is the inadequacy of the supporting data bases and the mistaken assumption the information they contained would be necessarily accurate. The misidentification of the targeted building as the [correct target] would not have occurred had the data bases had the correct location of the Chinese Embassy. All the data bases that contained information on the Chinese Embassy placed it at its original, pre-1996 location some four miles away. Thus, the question of possible damage to the Embassy was never a consideration.

**—George Tenet,
Former Director of Central Intelligence
Remarks to the House Permanent Select Committee
on Intelligence concerning the inadvertent Chinese
Embassy bombing, Operation ALLIED FORCE, 22 July**

The main targeting database resides in automated command and control tools (currently TBMCS). Problems with TBMCS have led targeteers in some theaters to build other databases. However, since the ATO is built using command/control tools, whatever database targeteers build must be interoperable with the C2 tools of record. Nonetheless, targeteers should realize that existing databases and systems often do not work properly. Having a backup system for target database management is necessary for the times when electronic systems fail.

DATUM MANAGEMENT

A datum is a mathematical model of the Earth used to calculate the coordinates on any map, chart, or survey system. There are many different datums that theaters can use for their geospatial intelligence needs. It is important that targeteers, especially those conducting point mensuration, understand the different datums that are used in theater. Certain aircraft utilize different datums in their on-board computers. Maps and charts use different datums as well. Point mensuration imagery may use other datums. Understanding the different datums is crucial for ensuring aircraft systems have the correct coordinates for munitions employment.

The possibility of targeting errors can greatly increase when different datums are used. During Operation DENY FLIGHT, units utilized maps and charts based on the ED-50 datum, some aircraft computers used the WGS-72 datum, and the J-2 provided target coordinates based on the WGS-84 datum. A specific coordinate plotted using a WGS-84 datum can be off by hundreds of meters if plotted using another datum. Such coordinate errors can result in devastating force employment errors, often resulting in attacking people and places that were not meant for attack. Errors can also be caused by discrepancies in vertical datums. Space-based systems, such as GPS and GPS-aided weapons, and imagery source material from sensors with space-based guidance provide coordinate elevations using the WGS-84 height above ellipsoid (HAE) datum. Most airborne navigation and littoral operations depend on mean sea level (MSL) altitudes and elevations. Both can be accurate, but the problem is that several methods to convert between HAE and MSL are in use. This often leads to conversion errors, which corrupts the HAE vertical component required in PGM tasking coordinates. In Afghanistan, garbled conversions caused problems for B-52s using joint direct attack munitions (JDAM) to attack cave entrances on vertical mountainsides.

Steps have been taken to prevent datum errors from happening. Chairman of the Joint Chiefs of Staff Instruction (CJCSI) 3900.01B has been drafted to clarify guidance on using both horizontal and vertical datums and standard coordinate and height formats for most operations. The NGA produces all new maps with the WGS-84 datum and in joint operations users must now reference horizontal and vertical coordinates to this datum. GPS also broadcasts its coordinates in this same datum. However, some possibility for error still exists. NGA reproduces certain older maps that use a WGS-72 datum. Also, if one is forced to use local maps, different countries use different datums. Most of the time, utilizing datum conversion software can minimize the possibility for error. In any case, targeteers should understand the different datums used in their theater prior to hostilities so measures can be taken to ensure accurate coordinates are provided to warfighters.

Limiting the number of datums used in theater is the obvious solution. However, as this is not always possible, especially in coalition operations, targeteers must be aware of the different datum needs of all the weapon systems that may be used in the operation.

ESTABLISHING CAOC RELATIONSHIPS

The units that make up the core of the CAOC are often assigned to various other organizations during peacetime. Operations, IOT, and logistics personnel are usually assigned to the theater AOG. Intelligence personnel are assigned to either the AOG or the theater A-2. Units must thus learn to coordinate their activities and perform their wartime CAOC functions in peacetime. This is especially important for targeting, since it cuts across CAOC divisional lines and involves a great deal of interaction with organizations outside the CAOC. As the primary "keepers" of targeting during peacetime, AIS targeteers must carefully establish relationships with these other units and agencies to ensure smooth targeting procedures are in place to support the tasking cycle during hostilities.

Combat Plans Squadron (CAOC combat plans and strategy divisions)

The CAOC's CPD "owns" targeting. Core CPD personnel reside in peacetime in the major command (MAJCOM) or numbered Air Force (NAF) combat plans squadron (CPS). However, members of the targeting and TA team within the ISRD carry out most targeting duties. Core ISRD personnel reside in peacetime in the MAJCOM or NAF AIS. As such, it is critical that targeting personnel in both the CPS and AIS routinely coordinate with each other during peacetime. This will ensure a smooth transition to working in a combat environment when the CAOC is officially stood up to support a contingency.

Most of the SD's core personnel also reside in the CPS in peacetime. Targeting personnel should be involved in the building of the campaign's air and space strategy and must coordinate with strategists in the CPS as strategy is developed.

Combat Operations Squadron (CAOC combat operations division)

Although the CPD "owns" targeting, targeting expertise is also needed in the CAOC's COD. This usually entails responding to changes in the ATO made necessary by changes in the tactical situation. Because of the extremely dynamic nature of activities in the COD, it is imperative that pre-coordination occur between the targeteers who will be working in the COD and the COD's ops planners. Such coordination is necessary to build the trust in personal knowledge and capabilities that such operations require.

Information Operations Flight/Squadron

These organizations offer depth of expertise about information operations in general. Such expertise is often spread to the other CAOC divisions for integration within specific CAOC processes. IOT personnel can assist targeteers in identifying key enemy nodes and in weaponeering and assessment for non-kinetic attacks.

ESTABLISHING FEDERATED AND REACHBACK RELATIONSHIPS

Targeting is, by nature, a cooperative effort. So is the intelligence support it requires. Neither can be accomplished without the aid of experts and agencies outside the CAOC. Both require reachback and federated support to be effective. Federation is the cooperative effort between the CAOC and/or COMAFFOR staff and all other Services and agencies (including joint and national) outside it. Reachback is a subset of federation; the cooperative effort between the CAOC and other Air Force agencies.

Peacetime AOGs and AIGs are not manned to provide all the expertise needed to support wartime targeting and assessment. Augmentees will fill out the CAOC when it stands up or readies itself for conflict, but the peacetime core of the organization must establish the federated and reachback relationships agencies needed to support their efforts. Even peacetime targeting demands will probably require daily coordination with agencies outside the CAOC, as they produce and consolidate analysis that supports theater air and space planning.

During peacetime, this coordination may be somewhat informal, as higher-level units provide intelligence to multiple users. However, combat demands much closer links and hence more formal coordination. The start of hostilities is not the time to begin solidifying these relationships. Many agencies support multiple theaters and have competing demands upon their time and effort. For this reason, proper coordination between CAOCs and other agencies is critical to ensure a continued, timely flow of pertinent intelligence. It is the responsibility of the CAOC to ensure these relationships are in place and that all federated and reachback partners understand their roles in how they support the CAOC's battle rhythm.

Federated and reachback relationships apply to both target development and assessment. Ideally, the organizations that support development of given targets or target systems should also conduct assessment on them during hostilities. The analysts that developed the targets already have a deep understanding of them and probably also developed MOE for them. However, manpower and tasking priorities will dictate if this is possible.

The number of units and agencies that can be called upon to lend reachback or federated support is staggering. There are literally thousands of analysts who, with proper coordination, can be called upon to support CAOC targeting and assessment in both peace and in war. See Appendix B for more information on these units and agencies.

EQUIPPING TARGETING ORGANIZATIONS

The forces the COMAFFOR presents to the CFC should include all the equipment they require to conduct combat operations. This includes target data and materials, especially for mission areas like strategic attack and counterair, which are conducted principally by the air and space component. The following sections discuss equipment considerations.

Analytical Tools

Targeting always requires solid intelligence analysis. While details are beyond the scope of this document, commanders must ensure that analysts and collection managers have the tools necessary to collect and analyze the information they need for targeting.

Geospatial Intelligence Tools

Geospatial intelligence (GEOINT) is the exploitation and analysis of imagery and geospatial information to describe, assess and visually depict physical features and geographically referenced activities on the earth. GEOINT is necessary for battlespace visualization, enabling planners to "see" natural and cultural features. The most basic geospatial intelligence tools are maps and charts. There are digital geospatial tools available for targeteers to use. Such tools provide a means of updating displays more accurately and conveniently than paper displays. Nonetheless, paper maps and charts are still in high demand and may become necessary if electronic means are somehow compromised. AOG/AIG intelligence directorates and A-staff A-2s must ensure that targeteers have access to appropriate digital tools and that adequate numbers of maps and charts are available for use by CAOC personnel.

Analysts also require mensuration tools to provide coordinates with the accuracy necessary for effective munitions employment. Point mensuration tools include the massive database of imagery needed for these activities. Large hard drives are necessary to store all these data. Point mensuration systems, software, and methodologies that do not utilize the digital point positioning data base and are not certified NGA standards are not approved to provide coordinates for GPS aided weapons.

Targeteers also need access to current imagery for target development and assessment. This is produced by many different units and distributed via the image product library system over Intelink. For more timely imagery, however, planners may need access to specific ISR systems. To fully exploit imagery, use of an electronic light table is necessary. In addition, commercial imagery may be available for use in targeting and assessment. The current commercial imagery system is Eagle Vision.

Weaponeering Tools

The JMEM is the standard reference for determining the munitions needed for an attack. The most effective tool from JMEM is the JMEM automated weaponeering system. Commanders must ensure adequate numbers of JMEM workstations are available for weaponeering. However, as non-kinetic and non-lethal weapons continue to make their way into the Air Force inventory, targeteers will have to expand their thinking of what weaponeering is. Commanders can assist by ensuring targeteers have tools to exploit such capabilities as they become available.

MAAP and "Operational Art" Tools

MAAP personnel need access to displays to aid in the development of the MAAP. Digital displays should be utilized to provide the wings and MAAP personnel with additional time for mission planning and significantly cuts down MAAP production time. Additionally, tools are available to automate some of the MAAP aircraft-munition-target matching effort. Any tools used should permit horizontal and vertical integration across functional areas in the OE.

Dynamic Targeting Tools

The highly fluid environment of the COD demands tools that targeteers can use to quickly and accurately respond to ATO changes. Typically, these tools are merely a reflection of the tools used by targeteers, analysts, and collection managers in the ISRD.

Collateral Damage Estimation Tools

Targeteers require a common tool allowing them to conduct collateral damage estimation and mitigation to ensure compliance with ROE and the LOAC.

TRAINING AND EXERCISES

There is no longer a specific Air Force Specialty Code for targeting. The only people who receive targeting training during technical school are intelligence personnel, but such training is only rudimentary and is not adequate for combat operations. Thus, it is imperative that targeteers in the CAOC receive appropriate follow-on training to achieve the level of proficiency needed for CAOC targeting. It is the responsibility of peacetime commanders to ensure *all* personnel involved in targeting understand their roles and duties. This applies to intelligence personnel as well as operators, weather personnel, IO specialists, and any others who are involved with CAOC targeting. It also includes federated and reachback partners. A number of courses provide training on targeting.

Formal Training

- ✪ **Combat Targeting Course (CTC)**. This Air Education and Training Command (AETC)-sponsored course is the Air Force's primary targeteer training course. Anyone working directly in the ISRD targeting and assessment team or the COD/CPD targeting team should consider this course

- ✪ **Joint Targeting School**. This US Joint Forces Command (USJFCOM)-sponsored course is another course for those who are working in ISRD and/or COD/CPD targeting. The joint targeting school provides a modern, joint perspective on targeting issues.

- ✪ **BDA Course**. This DIA-sponsored course provides the fundamentals of tactical assessment

- ✪ **Point mensuration training and certification program**. This program is an integral part of the geospatial point mensuration process and is required to build aim points for JDAM employment.

- ✪ **Collection Manager's Course**. This AETC-sponsored course is not specifically necessary for targeting. However, those involved with targeting will benefit by gaining an understanding of ISR collection assets, how they are tasked, and timelines for ISR asset tasking, collection, exploitation, and reporting

- ✪ **Information Warfare Applications Course**. This AETC-sponsored course is critical for information warfare (IW) specialists. As IW comes to play a larger role in Air Force operations, understanding of IW will become increasingly important, and nowhere more so than in targeting efforts

- ✪ **Weaponeering Mobile Training Teams**. These AETC-sponsored teams are available for those who cannot attend the combat training center or are in need of refresher training. Instructors travel to bases to conduct training, instead of requiring students to travel to Goodfellow AFB

Initial Qualification Training (IQT)

The Air Force has established a formal training unit for IQT of those filling CAOC positions. Located at Hurlburt Field, it was formally called the joint aerospace command and control course. This course will indoctrinate personnel into the inner workings of the CAOC. Targeting is addressed, but not explained in depth as it is in other specialized courses.

Mission Qualification Training (MQT)

Each standing CAOC (the MAJCOM or NAF's AOG, AIG, and/or AIS) is required to have an MQT program. MQT provides more in-depth training in CAOC processes, including targeting, as well as nuances specific to the theater.

Advanced Training

○ **Joint Air and Space Operations Planning Course**. This AETC-sponsored course trains participants how to develop a JAOP. Broad targeting concepts are addressed in the course. Attending the course provides insight for targeteers and analysts on the larger context of campaign planning

○ **Contingency Wartime Planning Course**. This AETC-sponsored course trains participants on the deliberate and crisis action planning processes, thus giving larger-context insight into those disciplines

○ **Command and Control Warrior's Advanced Course**. This Air Warfare Center-sponsored course provides "Master's" level CAOC training. Like CAOC formal training unit, the focus is on all CAOC processes, not just targeting

○ **USAF Weapons School (USAFWS)**. The mission of the USAFWS is to teach graduate-level instructor courses, which provide the world's most advanced training in weapons and tactical employment to officers in the combat air forces. (Also commonly know as the "WIC".)

Figure 5.1 Exercises vs. Reality

Exercises

The primary Air Force CAOC training exercise is BLUE FLAG, held three to four times a year. However, there are many other CAOC exercises, held by MAJCOMs, located throughout the world. Because many exercises use notional battlespace (e.g., the "Califon" scenario), it is important for targeteers (and other intelligence personnel) to be involved with the exercise planning at the earliest stages in order to inject as much realism as possible into the scenario. Constant coordination between targeteers, the combat plans squadron, and exercise A-Staff A-5 (Plans) is necessary to ensure exercise objectives and planning timelines are known.

It is often difficult to exercise the full targeting effort in C2-only exercises. For notional scenarios, target materials are not available and must be created, which is an extremely time consuming effort. Many times, target materials are simply not created at all. This severely limits the CAOC's ability to fully exercise targeting. In many cases targeting simply consists of management of a list of targets without any intelligence available to train planners on how and why certain targets are chosen for attack. Such "target servicing" is contrary to an effects-based approach and should be discouraged.

This lack of realism also harms assessment efforts. As the exercise runs, targets are simulated struck (or not). However, there is no imagery to correspond to strikes. All information that CAOC personnel would normally receive (INFLTREPs, MISREPs, imagery, SIGINT, etc.) is at best simulated by reports created electronically by the simulation. This can also result in negative training. Without a comprehensive game plan for training, targeteers and assessors will simply be regurgitating information produced by the simulation. Again, getting involved in the planning of the exercise at the earliest stage is critical if the exercise is to have as much realistic targeting and assessment training as possible.

It is critical that training be as realistic as possible. Airmen who learn operational art using fictional countries, with no live targets, no live ISR platforms, no real imagery, no real weapons risk, and without fully developing exercise targeting scenarios will not have adequate experience in targeting to be effective during wartime.

SUGGESTED READINGS

Air Force Publications
(NOTE: AFDDs and AFDC publications can be accessed via the HQ Air Force Doctrine Center website at https://www.doctrine.af.mil/Main.asp)

AFDD 2: *Operations and Organization*

AFDD 2-1: *Air Warfare*

AFDD 2-5: *Information Operations*

AFDD 2-8: *Command and Control*

AFDD 2-9: *Intelligence, Surveillance, and Reconnaissance Operations*

AFDD 2.1.2: *Strategic Attack*

AFDD 2-1.3: *Counterland*

AFDD 2-4.5: *Legal Support*

AFDCH 10-01: *Air and Space Commander's Handbook for the JFACC*

(NOTE: AFOTTPs can be accessed via the Air Warfare Center's AFOTTP web-site at https://505ccw.hurlburt.af.mil/505og/505os/AFOTTPLibrary.htm)

AFOTTP 2-1.1: *Air and Space Strategy*

AFOTTP 2-3.1: *USAF Command and Control Nodes*

AFOTTP 2-3.2: *Air and Space Operations Center*

AFOTTP 2-3.4: Joint Air and Space Operations Center

(NOTE: All other USAF publications can be accessed via the Air Force Publications web-site at http://www.e-publishing.af.mil)

AFI 13-1AOC V1: *Ground Environment Training – Air and Space Operations Center*

AFI 13-1AOC V2: *Standardization/Evaluation Program – Air and Space Operations Center*

AFI 13-1AOC V3: *Operational Procedures – Air and Space Operations Center*

AFI 14-117: *Air Force Targeting*

AFPAM 14-118: *Aerospace Intelligence Preparation of the Battlespace*

Joint Publications
(NOTE: Joint Publications can be accessed via the Joint Doctrine web-site at http://www.dtic.mil/doctrine/doctrine.htm)

JP 1-02: *DOD Dictionary of Military and Associated Terms*

JP 2-01: *Joint and National Intelligence Support to Military Operations*

JP 2-01.3: *Joint TTP for Joint Intelligence Preparation of the Battlespace*

JP 3-0: *Joint Operations*

JP 3-08: *Interagency, Intergovernmental Organization, and Nongovernmental Organization Coordination During Joint Operations*

JP 3-09: *Joint Fires*

JP 3-09.3: *Joint Tactics, Techniques, and Procedures for Close Air Support*

JP 3-13: *Information Operations*

JP 3-30: *Command and Control for Joint Air Operations*

JP 3-60: *Joint Targeting*

JP 5-0: *Joint Operation Planning*

JP 5-00.2: *Joint Task Force Planning Guidance and Procedures*

CJCSI 3900.01B, *Position Reference Procedures*

Other Publications
(NOTE: AU publications can be accessed via the Air University Press web-site at http://www.au.af.mil/au/aul/aupress)

Air Land Sea Applications Center, *Multi-Service TTP for Time-Sensitive Targets*. 2004.

Clausewitz, Carl von, *On War* (Princeton, NJ: Princeton University Press). 1976.

Defense Intelligence Agency, *DIA Battle Damage Assessment Quick Guide* (Washington, DC: US Government Printing Office (GPO)). 2003.

DOD, *Conduct of the Persian Gulf War: Final Report to Congress* (Chapter IV) (Washington, DC: US GPO). 1992.

Glock, John, "The Evolution of Air Force Targeting," *Airpower Journal*, Fall 1994 (Maxwell AFB, AL: Air University (AU) Press. 1994.

Headquarters, US Air Force, *The Air War Over Serbia: Aerospace Power in Operation ALLIED FORCE* (Washington DC: US GPO). 2000.

Mann, Edward, Gary Endersby, Thomas Searle, *Thinking Effects: Effects-Based Methodology for Joint Operations* (Maxwell AFB, AL: AU Press). 2002.

Meilinger, Phillip, editor, *The Paths of Heaven: The Evolution of Airpower Theory* (Maxwell AFB, AL: AU Press). 1997.

Rinaldi, Steven, *Beyond the Industrial Web: Economic Synergies and Targeting Methodologies* (Maxwell AFB, AL: AU Press). 1995.

Sun Tzu, *The Art of War* (Boulder, CO: Westview Press). 1994.

APPENDIX A

TARGETING AND LEGAL CONSIDERATIONS

INTRODUCTION

This appendix supports targeting by describing the various international legal obligations that impact upon targeting decisions. Legal considerations and international legal obligations directly affect all phases of targeting. Those involved in targeting should have a thorough understanding of these obligations and be able to apply them during the targeting analysis.

Specifically this appendix discusses briefly the legal considerations impacting targeting:

- Basic principles of the law of armed conflict (LOAC).
- LOAC considerations concerning personnel.
- LOAC considerations concerning objects and places.
- ROE considerations.
- "ROE-like" restrictions.

The last section outlines the role of judge advocates (JAs) in targeting.

Targeting must adhere to the LOAC and all applicable ROE. It is the policy of the DOD that the Armed Forces of the United States will comply with the law of war during all armed conflicts, however such conflicts are characterized, and, unless otherwise directed by competent authorities, the US Armed Forces will comply with the principles and spirit of the law of war during all other operations. The "law of war" is a term encompassing all international law for the conduct of hostilities binding on the United States including treaties and international agreements to which the United States is a party, and applicable customary international law. The "law of war" is also commonly referred to as the LOAC.

NOTE: This appendix is not all-encompassing. There may be instances that will be an exception to one of the listed legal considerations. These instances will be determined by the particular facts of a given situation and highlights the need for constant coordination between planners, operators and JAs.

BASIC PRINCIPLES OF LOAC AND THEIR TARGETING IMPLICATIONS

LOAC rests on four fundamental principles that are inherent to all targeting decisions: military necessity, unnecessary suffering, proportionality, and distinction (discrimination).

Military Necessity. *Is this target a valid "military objective"?* "Military necessity" acknowledges that attacks can be made against targets, but only targets that are valid "military objectives." In this case, the term "military objective" in this context comes from the description in the Additional Protocol to the Geneva Convention that describes military objectives as "…(T)hose objects by their nature, location, purpose or use make an effective contribution to military action…" Though the US is not a signatory to the Additional Protocol it views this definition as an accurate restatement of customary international law that we recognize and with which we comply.

NOTE: The word "objective" as used above should not be confused with the way "objective" is defined in the DOD Dictionary of Military Terms ("1. The clearly defined, decisive, and attainable goals towards which every military operation should be directed.")

For example, a residential home does not usually make an effective contribution to military action so is not usually a valid military target. However, there are instances and circumstances when something like a residence is a valid military target if an adversary is using it for military purposes (such as a military command post, a fighting position, etc.). In that case, the purpose or nature of the objective has been changed by the adversary's actions.

Unnecessary Suffering (Humanity). *Will the use of a particular weapon used to strike a target cause unnecessary suffering?* This principle is based in the Hague Conventions restrictions against using arms, projectiles, or materials calculated to cause *unnecessary* suffering. *All conventional weapons in the US inventory are permissible for use unless otherwise restricted by higher authority for operational reasons. These weapons have been reviewed to determine if they comply with the LOAC and have been determined not to cause unnecessary suffering when used in the manner in which they were designed.* However, this principle also prohibits using an otherwise lawful weapon in a manner that causes unnecessary suffering.

An example of causing unnecessary suffering would be to modify munitions to disperse glass projectiles to complicate providing medical treatment to the wounded. The bottom line is to use weapons and munitions as they are designed.

Proportionality. *Does the military advantage to be gained from striking a target outweigh the anticipated incidental civilian loss of life and property if this target is struck?* This requires the anticipated loss of civilian life and damage to civilian property incidental to attack is not excessive in relation to the concrete and direct military advantage expected from striking the target. Planners and commanders must weigh the expected military advantages to be gained from affecting a target (kinetic or non-kinetic) against the incidental loss or injury to civilians and the damage or destruction of civilian property. The "military advantage anticipated" refers to the advantage anticipated from those actions considered as a whole, and not only from isolated or particular actions. A "military advantage" is not just a tactical gain, but can span the spectrum of tactical, operational, or strategic.

For example, an armored vehicle used in combat is located at a school. The vehicle is a valid target. However, destroying the vehicle with certain types of munitions may place lives and safety of nearby noncombatants in jeopardy. The potential for injury to noncombatants should help guide the choice of munitions and/or other actions chosen against the vehicle.

Distinction (Discrimination). *Have we distinguished between combatants and non-combatants; have we distinguished between military objectives and protected property or places?* The principle, based on customary international law, requires parties to direct operations only against combatants and military objectives. It prohibits "indiscriminate attacks".

For example: Dropping munitions—guided or not—in a residential area without regard to whether there are combatants or military objectives in the area simply because there "might be" adversary forces there would be an indiscriminate attack. The use of gravity-guided munitions (non-precision) against enemy combatants or military objectives is not of itself an indiscriminate attack.

LOAC TARGETING RESTRICTIONS

Personnel

Are we targeting personnel protected under LOAC? Intentional direct attacks on civilians are prohibited. However, this is distinctly different from the incidental injury that may be caused to civilians or civilian objects as a result of an attack on a valid military target (collateral damage). Collateral damage is an issue of proportionality.

Protection of the Civilian Population. Civilian populations may not be intentionally targeted for attack. Acts of violence designed to spread terror among the civilian population are prohibited. However, civilians may not be used as "human shields" to protect military targets from attack. The fact that they may be used to do so does not necessarily prevent the military object from being attacked. As directed or time permitting, targets surrounded by human shields will probably need to be reviewed by higher authority for policy and legal considerations based on the specific facts.

Protection of Wounded and Sick. Direct attacks on wounded and sick who are no longer contributing to an adversary's military operations are prohibited by the Geneva Conventions. As noted above, the incidental additional injury that might be caused to sick and wounded still on the battlefield in the proximity to valid military targets is an issue of proportionality. The sick and wounded may also not be used as "human shields" to protect military targets from attack. The fact that they may be used to do so does not necessarily prevent the military object from being attacked. As directed or time permitting, targets surrounded by human shields will probably need to be reviewed by higher authority for policy and legal considerations based on the specific facts.

Protection of Prisoners of War. Direct attacks on prisoners of war (POW) are also prohibited by the Geneva Conventions. This occurs from the moment they have surrendered because they are no longer considered "combatants" at that point. POW camps or detention facilities should be marked to be visible from the air as such. However, it is important that any POW facility is also noted as such on a NSL to ensure there is no confusion on the part of aircrew between the POW facility and adversary forces that may be conducting rear-area operations.

Objects and Places

Are we targeting an object or place protected under LOAC? Intentional direct attacks on civilian objects are prohibited. However, this is distinct from the incidental injury that may be caused to civilian objects as a result of an attack on a valid military target. Likewise, there are instances when based on the facts of a particular situation a civilian object may be a valid military target. These are discussed below.

Protection of Civilian Objects. Civilian objects may not be intentionally targeted for attack. Civilian objects are civilian property and facilities *other than* those used to support or sustain the adversary's warfighting capability. Civilian objects that are being used to engage in or support hostilities may lose their protected civilian status and be legitimate military targets.

Civilian objects that may be legitimate military targets. Some facilities or objects that might be considered as civilian objects but are actually legitimate military targets based on the facts surrounding their nature, location, purpose, and use:

a. **Dual-Use Objects.** These are facilities or objects that serve both a military and civilian purpose and may be legitimate military targets. For example a power grid that supports an enemy airbase, but also supports civilian cities/towns is dual-use, but might be considered a legitimate military target. A target such as this would need to be examined in light of "proportionality" concerning whether targeting the power grid would be disproportionate to the effects caused to the surrounding civilian objects supported by the same power grid. Typically dual-use targets will require a higher level of approval authority because of the concerns on the impact on the civilian population.

b. **Economic Objects.** These are typically factories, workshops and plants that make an effective (though not necessarily direct) contribution to an adversary's military capability. Like dual-use targets, these typically require a higher level of approval because of the particular facts and circumstances regarding the nature, location, use, and purpose of the target.

c. **Lines of Communication.** Transportation systems (roadways, bridges, etc) and communication systems (TV, radio), while civilian in nature, may also be considered legitimate military targets based on their use. Like dual-use and economic objects, these may require higher level of approval based on the particular facts and circumstances regarding nature, location, use, and purpose of the target.

Protection of Medical Units, Hospitals, and Medical Transport. Under the Geneva Conventions, these are not to be attacked. These should be marked by a distinctive medical emblem such as the Red Cross, Red Crescent, or some other internationally recognized symbol to show that they are for medical use. Known medical facilities and structures will typically be placed in the combatant commander's no-strike list database. Like civilian personnel, these may not be used to shield legitimate military targets. For instance, placing a surface-to-air missile (SAM) system next to a hospital does not prevent an attack on the SAM system if necessary in self-defense. Usually the combatant commander will issue guidance concerning the approval authority for mobile systems placed next to such protected objects when not acting in self-defense.

Protection of Religious, Cultural, and Charitable Buildings and Monuments. Under the Hague Conventions, international treaties and customary law, buildings and monuments devoted to religion, art, charitable purposes, or historical sites are not to be attacked. These should be marked with internationally recognized distinctive emblems (such as the blue shield with two white triangles). Known buildings and monuments devoted to religious, cultural, and charitable purposes will typically be placed in the combatant commander's "no-strike list" database. "Cultural" properties are usually considered irreplaceable and the property of all mankind. Like civilians, these may not be used to shield legitimate military targets. For instance, placing a SAM in the ruins of an ancient temple would not prevent an attack on the SAM system if necessary in self-defense. Usually the combatant commander will issue guidance concerning the approval authority for striking mobile systems placed next to such protected buildings or monuments when not in self-defense.

RULES OF ENGAGEMENT

Have applicable restrictions or requirements imposed by the ROE been complied with prior to striking a target? The ROE are directives issued by competent military authority to delineate the circumstances and limitations under which air, ground, and naval forces will initiate or continue combat engagement with other forces encountered. (JP 1-02, *DOD Dictionary of Military and Associated Terms*). *Essentially, ROE are rules for a particular operation that govern the use of force to reflect the will of the civilian and military leadership.* ROE constrain the actions of US military forces to ensure their actions are consistent with domestic and international law, national policy, and objectives. Although ROE are not law, they are <u>authoritative</u> restrictions issued at the appropriate level of command to control the use of force. ROE are based on domestic and international law, history, strategy, political concerns, and a vast wealth of operational wisdom, experience, and knowledge provided by military commanders and operators. ROE may be more *restrictive* than the LOAC for a given situation, but they can't be more *permissive* than allowed under LOAC—therefore compliance with ROE should guarantee compliance with LOAC.

Personnel involved in targeting should be involved in the development and refinement of ROE along with the judge advocates. Just as tasking and targeting are cyclical, so too is ROE development, and it may require constant input and refinement in order to meet operational requirements.

What is contained in ROE. There is usually information in the ROE that is directly applicable to how, when, or under what circumstances targets may be struck. The ROE may contain such information as target approval authorities for certain types or classes of targets (e.g., economic objects, lines of communication), and approval authority for time-sensitive or high-collateral damage targets. It may also contain information regarding what weapons may be used, (like cluster bombs or anti-personnel mines) the conditions for use and approval authority for their use.

Where ROE Are Found. ROE may be found in the standing rules of engagement (SROE), a combatant commander's theater-specific ROE, and ROE issued specifically for an operation (such as with Operations ENDURING FREEDOM and IRAQI FREEDOM).

a. **Standing Rules of Engagement.** These are contained in a classified Joint Chiefs of Staff Instruction. The SROE provide implementation guidance on the inherent right of self-defense and the application of force for mission accomplishment. The SROE also provide a framework for the development and implementation of ROE across the spectrum of military operations. The important point to remember is that the SROE are not tailored to specific military operations. They provide guidance in the absence of operation-specific ROE, and do not contain specific targeting restrictions or considerations based on the circumstances of a particular operation.

b. **Theater-Specific Rules of Engagement.** These are the combatant commanders' theater-specific ROE. These ROE address specific strategic and political sensitivities of the AOR, and must be approved by the Chairman of the Joint Chiefs of Staff. Theater-specific ROE may have been issued in a separate message. Like the SROE, these will not provide specific targeting restrictions or considerations based on ongoing operational constraints.

c. **Operation-Specific ROE.** These ROE are promulgated by the President, Secretary of Defense, combatant commander and component commanders and are based upon the specific factors underlying the operation. The ROE might be sent to the components via message from the combatant commander or could be incorporated into the OPORD. *The ROE are usually re-stated in the JAOP and in Section Five of the air and space component's daily SPINS.*

ROE Considerations. For examples of the kinds of issues to be considered in ROE development, refer to AFDD 2-4.5, *Legal Support*, Chapter Three (Legal Support for Rules of Engagement) and to AFDCH 10-01, *Air and Space Commander's Handbook for the JFACC* (ROE appendix).

a. **AFDD 2-4.5,** *Legal Support,* **ROE Chapter**. This chapter provides guidance in how to develop ROE. Considerations discussed include: ROE development is a collaborative effort (vertical and horizontal among organizations); ROE development *must* integrate all players (JA, commanders, planners, operators); ROE should not be too specific or restrictive; and ROE need to provide simple, clear guidance to accomplish the mission.

b. **Air and Space Commander's Handbook for the JFACC.** This handbook is a quick "spin up" reference and focuses on CFACC effectiveness. Considerations discussed in the appendix include: ROE requires mission analysis; ROE development is an integral part of operational planning; and ROE should not substitute for guidance, intent and judgment.

"ROE-like" Restrictions Impacting Targeting

Are there any other restrictions that may impact targeting? Restrictions that are not formally issued as ROE may exist in other documents. In theory, these would be explicitly incorporated in the ROE or at least incorporated by reference. In practice, this is not always the case. As such, it is imperative that all personnel involved in targeting work—operators, planners and judge advocates—ensure they are aware of *all* applicable targeting restrictions regardless of how these restrictions are characterized or issued. Some examples are listed below.

Target Lists. The NSL, RTL, and JTL are compiled and maintained by the combatant command. An NSL will contain those facilities and structures that are protected under LOAC (churches, hospitals, etc). The RTL contains facilities and structures for which approval must first be obtained from the establishing authority before striking. These are on the RTL because there is some function or valid military reason for why it should not be struck. Targets on the JTL may also contain restrictions in the target folders. Although a target itself may be approved for strike and placed on the JTL, its target folder may restrict specific DPIs from being struck or restrict the size or type of munitions that may be used against the target or some of its DPIs. For example, if a target is near a sensitive site, such as a school, the DPIs closest to the school may be restricted entirely or restricted to only certain types of weapons.

Collateral Damage Methodology (CDM). Historically, various combatant commands have conducted CDM according to their own standards. Joint Chiefs of Staff directives now delineate a coherent five-step process that standardizes DOD CDM practices.

The JAOP. Many restrictions from the combatant commander, CFC, and the CFACC will be found in sections of the JAOP that set forth standing orders or commander's intent.

Special Instructions. SPINs are periodically issued by the CAOC and usually have several sections that may contain ROE. Most SPINs have a subsection specifically called "ROE" that may contain ROE changes until a new version or regular changes to the OPORD can be published. This section will also contain any amplification the CFACC deems necessary for complex ROE provisions.

Fragmentary Orders (FRAGO). In some past operations, restrictions from the combatant commander impacting targeting were also published in FRAGOs.

Fire Support Annex. The fire support annex to an OPORD may also contain additional guidance or information concerning targeting.

Coalition Concerns. Coalition forces may have their own set of ROE that may not be similar to US ROE. That may impact whether coalition forces have the authority to strike certain sensitive targets such as leadership, WMD, etc. or the type of support they are able to provide to US forces striking those targets. US forces operating from coalition bases (e.g., Diego Garcia) may also have restrictions placed on them—and on the targeting they execute—by coalition ROE as well. Close coordination is required with coalition partners during targeting to facilitate the understanding of their ROE and the limits it may impose on them.

ROLE OF THE JUDGE ADVOCATE

So what does the JA have to do with targeting? The JA assists the planners and operators with reviewing targets for compliance with applicable LOAC/ROE restrictions (including collateral damage and other combatant commander restrictions) prior to mission execution. Legal advice and counsel is necessary to the development, interpretation, modification, and proper implementation of the ROE. JAs and their support staff should be trained, operationally oriented, and readily accessible to assist planners and operators with international legal considerations and ROE or related issues. JAs have an affirmative duty to provide legal advice to commanders and their staffs that is consistent with the international and domestic legal obligations and the governing ROE. The complexity of international legal considerations along with the ROE requires JAs to be available at all stages in the tasking cycle. JAs are usually available 24/7 to the strategy, plans and operations divisions within an CAOC. Additionally, JAs are usually available at the expeditionary wing and group level to assist commanders, aircrew, and planners at the tactical level with targeting-related issues at that level. It should be emphasized, however, that inputs and counsel provided by the JA and staff are advisory rather than authoritative. Legal considerations must be weighed against military necessity, imminent threat, and/or operational gain by the CFACC and CFC.

APPENDIX B

FEDERATED SUPPORT TO TARGETING AND ASSESSMENT

We [at United States Strategic Command] provided federated intelligence support to multiple regional combatant commands, conducting battle damage assessment and intelligence analysis, and leading the intelligence community-wide effort to find and characterize underground facilities in Afghanistan.

—Admiral James Ellis
Commander, United States Strategic Command
Remarks to the House Armed Services Committee, 13 Mar 03

INTRODUCTION

Targeting and assessment requirements are typically more than theaters can support internally, due to deficiencies in manpower and specialized expertise. Thus, in practice, targeting is federated among many different organizations—in the theater, in the US, and worldwide. The COMAFFOR may have direct authority over some units, but will not have control over other targeting organizations. It is therefore crucial that theater strategists, planners, and targeteers develop the necessary relationships with these units and organizations during peacetime so that intelligence support to targeting and assessment will flow smoothly during contingencies. While theater targeting units can seldom, if ever, directly task federated organizations, they can develop working relationships through which these organizations can provide support the theater needs.

The key to an effective federation system is knowing the capabilities of the various units and organizations—Air Force, joint, and national—that can be called upon for support. There are many organizations that can and do produce intelligence and other information useful to theater targeting and assessment efforts. Such expertise has always been important, but it is essential for an effects-based approach to conflict, which relies on greater SA, more comprehensive planning, and deeper knowledge of the adversary than an attrition-based approach does.

CAOC strategists, planners, targeteers, and intelligence analysts are generalists in the sense that they must have knowledge of a wide variety of weapon, target, and political systems. Federated targeting organizations have specialists with extensive knowledge on specific target systems in specific nations. Utilizing this expertise is absolutely necessary if targeteers are to conduct effective target development that imposes the specific effects chosen by planners to achieve commanders' objectives.

There are many kinds of information available to support targeting and assessment efforts. Traditional approaches to both have emphasized imagery intelligence—usually overhead imagery from satellites and reconnaissance aircraft. While imagery is certainly still important, other "INTs" such as HUMINT, SIGINT, measurement and signature intelligence (MASINT), foreign instrumentation signals intelligence (FISINT), and open-source intelligence (OSINT); can be equally—and sometimes more— important to targeteers and planners. Collaboration with federated organizations will enable analysts to pull together this multitude of intelligence to utilize in targeting.

Federation Classification

We need to do a better job of human intelligence. There are some things that you are just not going to see from space. Overhead imagery is very important, but we should not over-emphasize it. They [potential adversaries] know how to conceal the imagery, and that won't give us the complete picture.

—Dr. Stephen Younger,
Director, Defense Threat Reduction Agency (DTRA)
Comments concerning intelligence support
for precision strike capabilities, 2004

There are two fundamental ways to classify federated support, which affect how relationships are built, help determine how taskings are conveyed, and influence how information is disseminated. All components—Air Force and joint, official and unofficial—are required for effective federation.

Air Force and Joint/National. CAOC planners are concerned with two federated systems: one internal to the Air Force (also known as "reachback") and one that involves joint and national agencies. The Air Force only has control over the reachback system. The joint/national system is based on the needs of geographic combatant commanders or CFCs. These needs are coordinated with the larger joint community through the Joint Staff J-2's deputy director for targeting (J2T). However, the COMAFFOR should submit requirements through the combatant commander or CFC for any joint or national federated support he or she needs. In both cases, federated support should be coordinated prior to hostilities. Such coordination should delineate specific duties to federated partners, establish timelines, and determine the methods of communication to be used. Additionally, whenever possible, COMAFFORs should coordinate federated partner participation in theater exercises. Without proper coordination, federated partners may be unclear of duties once hostilities begin. Exercise participation may reveal points of friction, process errors, and operational limitations that coordination alone may not reveal. Federated partners may also have conflicting priorities if multiple contingencies occur simultaneously in different theaters, as most federated partners are not subordinate to a single, specific theater and solid peacetime working relationships may help reduce the impact of such seams or priority conflicts.

Official and Unofficial. Targeting and assessment are year-round efforts. In the past, many organizations supported theater targeting efforts even though they were not officially part of a federated team. This support was often slow, due to limitations of existing communication technology. Development of the internet and creation of Intelink, however, ushered in a whole new era of federated partnership. Much of the intelligence that was created for and sent to specific theaters in years past is now disseminated to the world via the net. Peacetime federation, therefore, is often informal. During hostilities, however, formal relationships are necessary, since timelines are severely reduced. For instance, NGA produce daily imagery for use in target development. They produce this imagery because that is what sensors have taken pictures of. CAOC planners can coordinate with NGA to obtain these products, but they require no formal relationship to do so. While the intelligence community is doing its mission, the CAOC is simply taking advantage of available resources. During a conflict, however, the CAOC's needs may require specific NGA action and be much more time-critical. This may require a formal request for support from the CFC to the NGA. Obviously, if the need can be anticipated and planned for, the partners can accomplish the necessary requests and coordination, which will improve the timeliness and quality of the support. The bottom line is that, while peacetime requirements may be met a less formal federated structure, contingencies dictate that all federation partners know exactly what support is required of them, the timelines involved with providing the support, and in what manner they need to provide it.

Types of Federated Support

Federated partners can provide support to many stages of targeting.

Objectives, effects, and guidance. Many federated organizations, both Air Force and joint, have analysts who have studied specific targets, target sets, nations, and regions for many years. Many of the analysts with deepest understanding are civilians working for national intelligence agencies. Their comprehensive expertise may be useful to CAOC strategists when developing objectives, effects, and measures of effectiveness.

Target Development. Federated targeting units conduct target development year-round. Theater targeting units can utilize this information, reducing redundancy as well as workload. There are a large number of intelligence and other analytic organizations that specialize in certain targets or target systems. For instance, the Air Force Information Warfare Center (AFIWC) can provide information on command and control linkages; the Joint Warfare Analysis Center (JWAC) has engineers who specialize in lines of communication, electrical power generation, and POL distribution; and DIA's Missile and Space Intelligence Center (MSIC) are experts in surface-to-air missiles. These, and many other organizations, can be called upon to provide expertise for specific targeting efforts. Even if these organizations are not official members of a theater federated targeting effort, they can still be utilized to assist with target development.

Collateral Damage Estimation. While CAOC personnel can conduct most of the effort required to estimate collateral damage, some estimates require advanced estimation methods that only national organizations have expertise in. JWAC and the Defense Threat Reduction Agency (DTRA), for example, have specialists who can assist in this effort.

Weaponeering. Many units specialize in weaponeering for specific munitions or target categories. For instance, the 20th Intelligence Squadron at Offutt AFB specializes in weaponeering for hardened and deeply buried targets. Targeteers at USSTRATCOM specialize in similar activities. Weaponeering is time-consuming; utilizing federated partners to conduct weaponeering frees CAOC planners to focus on other critical planning activities.

Point mensuration. Federated partners can assist CAOCs with point mensuration. Because it is so time consuming, mensuration may overwhelm CAOC targeteers. Many Air Force and joint units, especially NGA, can provide expertise in this area.

Assessment. Partners can assist CAOCs in determining appropriate MOE and in analyzing collected data. Joint and national agencies may be particularly useful in helping make political and economic types of assessment. Ideally, the same units that provide support for target development should also assist with the post-attack assessment of those targets and target sets, regardless of the means of attack. Obviously, analysts who support target development will already have detailed knowledge that can be put to use during assessment. Establishing federated relationships early will help ensure this happens.

The preceding list is not all-inclusive. CAOC targeteers should understand and utilize all federated specialties available. Understanding the capabilities of all possible federated partners will provide insight into the types of support that are available for use throughout all CAOC processes.

THEATER ORGANIZATIONS

There are numerous organizations that may be called upon to support theater targeting and assessment efforts. It is imperative that CAOC targeteers understand the organizations that they can utilize to support CAOC targeting efforts...both in peacetime and during wartime.

Air Force Units

Core CAOC. There are two core units that support targeting for most CAOCs: the AOG and the AIS. IOTs also support targeting and are integral to AOG. In addition, theaters have two supporting intelligence units: the distributed ground system and the information operations group. Further, the director of space forces may be of assistance in coordinating space requirements in support of targeting.

The majority of Air Force targeteers are assigned to Air Force component AIS' and they provide the lion's share of input to the targeting effort. However, AOG CPS personnel form the core of the targeting effort. Some AIS' are organizationally subordinate to the MAJCOM or NAF AOGs. Other AIS' are subordinate to a NAF Air Intelligence Group. Regardless, these are peacetime organizations. During contingencies, AIS' "become" the ISRD of their corresponding CAOCs.

Deployable Common Ground System (DCGS). The AF has developed specific units to provide enhanced intelligence and targeting support for worldwide operations— above what the theater AIS can provide. DCGS is the system and the individual units are called Deployable Ground Systems (DGS). While these units do not provide support directly to targeteers, they do provide SIGINT and imagery support to theater CAOCs that ultimately supports targeting and assessment. CAOCs should coordinate DGS support through the theater A-2.

There are currently five operational DGS'. While they each have a primary theater, the DCGS operates as a single entity and specific DGS' can be called upon to flex from their primary theater to support a more critical area, as warfighter needs dictate. Targeteers must keep this in mind when coordinating DGS reachback support to the CAOC. While not officially part of a theater CAOC, these units can provide invaluable IMINT and SIGINT support to CAOC IPB, targeting, collection management, and assessment efforts.

Joint and National Organizations

Joint Units

Theater Joint Intelligence Operations Center or Joint Analysis Center (JAC). The theater JIOC (or JAC in US European Command) is the central point for theater intelligence tasking, collection, analysis, and production. JIOCs also have targeting offices that produce target folders based on deliberate planning taskings. In addition, JIOCs, in coordination with theater J-2s, maintain the JTL, NSL, and RTL for specific OPLANs or CONPLANs. JIOCs have liaisons from the major national intelligence agencies to facilitate effective national intelligence support to the theaters. These liaisons typically include personnel from DIA, NGA, the National Security Agency (NSA), and the Central Intelligence Agency (CIA) (the roles of these organizations are explained later in this appendix).

Theater Cruise Missile Support Agency (CMSA). CMSA-Pacific (Camp Smith, Hawaii) and CMSA-Atlantic (Norfolk, Virginia) can provide valuable targeting information for cruise missile employment (airborne and seaborne).

Global Cryptologic Center (GCC). A GCC is an NSA site to ensure NSA-derived intelligence supports theater planning, force employment, and assessment. CAOC planners can coordinate with the GCC or go through the theater NSA representative at the JIOC (the cryptologic support group); but a theater can't directly task an GCC—it must go through NSA. However, air and space planners can consult with their theater's supporting GCC. There are three US-based GCCs, each with a focus on a specific theater, or multiple theaters.

National Intelligence Support Team (NIST). A NIST is a team composed of personnel from DIA, NSA, NGA, CIA, or other national intelligence agencies that is deployed, upon request by a CFC, to facilitate the flow of timely all-source intelligence between his joint task force (JTF) and Washington during crises or contingency operations. The NIST concept is designed to create a dynamic flow of intelligence to and from the JTF operational area. The NIST provides reachback to national intelligence agencies and provides the CFC and his staff with knowledge of each agency's resources and capabilities that normally does not exist at the JTF level. Team members provide a direct agency liaison for the JTF, and have an understanding of where to go in their parent agency to obtain the best support for the commanders' priority intelligence requirements.

AIR FORCE CONTINENTAL US-BASED SUPPORT ORGANIZATIONS

Headquarters USAF

HQ USAF. AF/A2 and A3I are the focal points for coordinating the Air Force's CONUS-based targeting and assessment reachback support.

Air Force Network Operations and Security Center (AFNOSC). The AFNOSC provides the commander of Air Force network operations the means to ensure the security, integrity, and timely delivery of ISR information transiting the Air Force enterprise network. The AFNOSC directs activities of the Regional NOSCs and wing-level network control centers to ensure integrity of the Air Force segment of the global information grid. Health of the network directly impacts targeting capability.

Air Combat Command (ACC)

ACC Intelligence Directorate (ACC/A2) plays a large part in coordinating the Air Force's CONUS-based reachback support, as many organizations involved are subordinate to ACC. As the analytical arm of the A2 staff, the ACC intelligence squadron will factor into the federated process.

Operational or Intelligence Wings. There are currently several units that provide worldwide targeting support, helping to develop target planning products and geospatial intelligence materials for strike missions across the globe. These units maintain the only DOD-controlled image base production entity outside the NGA, collecting satellite and airborne imagery from commercial sources. Other functions include peacetime supervision of theater IOTs and some elements of non-continental US (CONUS) DGS units, and coordinating the Air Force's tactics and reporting program. Headquarters ACC can provide commanders and planners more information concerning what the various units are and what functions they perform.

Air Force Information Warfare Center is the Air Force center of excellence for IO. AFIWC produces IO analyses and data for combat operations and targeting (and acquisition programs as well). It also assesses IO vulnerabilities of units and conducts adversary IO operation and vulnerability assessments.

National Air and Space Intelligence Center (NASIC) is the sole national center for integrated intelligence analysis on air and space systems, forces, and threats. It assesses current and projected foreign air and space capabilities and intentions, develops targeting and mission planning intelligence materials, and evaluates evolving technologies of potential adversaries. Such technical information is useful in determining how to create specific effects on specific targets and target systems. In addition to expertise on worldwide air assets, NASIC also has leading experts on long-range surface-to-surface missiles (such as medium-range and intercontinental ballistic missiles).

Air Force Space Command

Air Force Space Command has deep expertise in space operations. Such information can prove useful when analyzing and targeting enemy space capabilities. Targeteers at the joint space operations center (JSpOC) evaluate theater AODs and nominate specific space-related targets to meet a theater commander's objectives. Their expertise is invaluable when analyzing and targeting enemy space capabilities.

Air Mobility Command (AMC)

AMC Intelligence maintains databases on airfields worldwide in the event AMC must utilize those bases. Such information may be useful when targeting enemy airfields.

Air Force Materiel Command

Air Armaments Center (AAC) is responsible for the development, acquisition, testing, deployment, and sustainment of all non-nuclear air-delivered weapons. The information they provide may be beneficial during weaponeering and conducting munitions effectiveness assessments.

JOINT AND NATIONAL CONUS-BASED SUPPORT ORGANIZATIONS

Joint Chiefs of Staff (JCS)

J-2 Intelligence Directorate, Deputy Director for Targeting (J2T). The J-2 is the national level focal point for crisis intelligence to support military operations as well as indications and warning. J2T is the coordinator for all joint and national federation needs of a unified command or JTF. CAOC targeteers should coordinate their federation needs with the MAJCOM or NAF A-2, who will then coordinate with the

CFC's J-2. However, the CAOC should first determine which of its needs can be met by utilizing Air Force reachback partnerships.

National Agencies

Defense Intelligence Agency. The JCS J-2 is dual-hatted as the Director of DIA. DIA is a major producer and manager of foreign military intelligence with a worldwide outlook. DIA is normally the first stop when analysts need foreign military intelligence to support targeting and assessment. In addition to the main DIA Center in Washington, DC, DIA maintains two specialized intelligence centers:

✪ **Missile and Space Intelligence Center** provides worldwide scientific and technical intelligence concerning threat guided missile systems, directed energy weapons, selected space programs/systems and related C2 to support operationally deployed forces. MSIC has experts knowledgeable on SAMs as well as short-range ballistic missiles.

✪ **Armed Forces Medical Intelligence Center (AFMIC)** produces finished, all-source medical intelligence in support of military planning and operations. Assessments, forecasts, and databases are prepared on worldwide infectious disease occurrence, global environmental health risks, foreign military and civilian health care capabilities and trends, and militarily significant life science technologies.

National Geospatial-Intelligence Agency is the primary national producer of geospatial-intelligence, which is the exploitation and analysis of imagery and geospatial information to describe, assess, and visually depict physical features and geographically referenced activities on the earth. Products include controlled imagery, digital elevation data and selected feature information, which can be rapidly augmented and fused with other spatially referenced information such as intelligence, weather, and logistics data resulting in an integrated, digital view of the mission space. NGA also produces many of the maps and charts Airmen utilize for mission planning.

National Security Agency employs mathematicians, linguists, engineers, and computer scientists focusing on information assurance (code making) and SIGINT (code breaking). NSA's code breakers collect, process, analyze, and exploit foreign adversaries' communications. NSA maintains its headquarters at Fort Meade, Maryland. However, it also has three regional centers, each with a regional focus.

Defense Threat Reduction Agency is a combat support agency charged with developing methods to deal more effectively with threats by nuclear, radiological, chemical, biological, and high explosive weapons of mass destruction and preventing future threats. The agency focuses DOD efforts to prepare for and respond to WMD attacks. These technologies provide commanders options for effective targeting against enemy WMD capabilities, WMD delivery methods, and underground or hardened structures, as well as enhanced capabilities to assess enemy WMD operations.

Defense Information Systems Agency (DISA) is a combat support agency responsible for planning, engineering, acquiring, fielding, and supporting global net-centric solutions and operating the defense information system network. DISA seeks to guarantee our forces global information dominance by providing jointly interoperable systems that have assured security, survivability, availability, and superior quality. Because of DISA's expertise in developing, maintaining and protecting US information methods, they may prove useful in developing targeting strategies to attack enemy information methods and systems.

Unified Commands

Functional Unified Command Joint Intelligence Centers. The four CONUS-based functional unified commands—USSTRATCOM, USJFCOM, US Transportation Command (USTRANSCOM), and US Special Operations Command (USSOCOM)—each has a JIOC. Each of these unified commands has a global outlook and, as such, is capable of providing targeting and assessment support to combatant commands worldwide in the areas of special operations, transportation, WMD, space, nuclear forces, and information warfare, to name a few.

Joint Warfare Analysis Center. Subordinate to USJFCOM, JWAC provides planners with specialized lines of communications analysis for use in developing targeting strategies. JWAC provides innovative and accurate engineering and modeling-based targeting options with an understanding of risks and consequences, including collateral damage estimates.

Joint Information Operations Center. Subordinate to USSTRATCOM, this center is responsible for the integration of IO into military plans and operations across the spectrum of conflict. The center provides direct command and control warfare (C2W) tactical and technical analytical support to operational commanders. The center supports the integration of operations security, psychological operations, military deception, electronic warfare and destruction throughout the planning and execution phases of the operations. Direct support is provided to unified commands, JTFs, functional and service components, and subordinate combat commanders. The center maintains specialized expertise in C2W systems engineering, operational applications, capabilities and vulnerabilities.

Joint Space Operations Center (JSpOC). JSpOC is the primary USSTRATCOM interface for space effects to the supported commander, to include all aspects of deliberate planning, crisis action planning, adaptive campaign planning and the air tasking cycle. The JSpOC is responsible for analyzing and targeting enemy space capabilities in support of theaters in addition to their global mission. JSpOC targeteers can evaluate theater AODs and nominate specific space-related targets to meet a theater commander's objectives

Joint Technical Coordinating Group for Munitions Effectiveness (JTCG/ME) is a vital joint service activity that develops operational effectiveness estimates for all non-nuclear munitions and continuously updates JMEMs used by the Services for training and tactics development, operational targeting, weapons selection, aircraft loadouts, and planning for ammunition procurement, survivability, and development of improved munitions. JTCG/ME directs the analytical effort of working groups necessary to determine degrading effects of various terrain environments on non-nuclear munitions effectiveness and improving the database for target vulnerability, delivery accuracy, and weapons characteristics. JTCG/ME promotes and develops standardized procedures and models used by the Services and the munitions industry for the evaluation of non-nuclear munitions effectiveness and conducts special studies concerning munitions effectiveness.

JTCG/ME is managed through the JTCG/ME program office within the Army Materiel Systems Analysis Activity at Aberdeen Proving Grounds, Maryland. Part-time participants from the various Services are organized into working groups that represent the major areas of interest. These groups include air-to-surface, surface-to-surface, anti-air, target standardization, special effects, and information operations. Principal Service members serve on the JTCG/ME steering committee to direct group activities and funding. The US Army, as lead Service, appoints the steering committee chairman.

Sister Services

The US Army maintains an intelligence collection and analysis structure that Airmen may utilize when conducting many air and space operations. The Intelligence and Security Command (INSCOM) provides a wide variety of ground-based intelligence through its main production center, the National Ground Intelligence Center (NGIC).

The US Navy also maintains an intelligence collection, analysis, and production structure that Airmen may utilize when conducting many air and space operations. Because the Navy's "forward from the sea" concept and its large airpower capability, US Navy intelligence has a focus in many ways similar to Air Force intelligence. There are three main organizations that Airmen can utilize for targeting and assessment support. The Office of Naval Intelligence's (ONI) main production center is the National Maritime Intelligence Center (NMIC).

US Marine Corps, through the Marine Corps Intelligence Activity (MCIA), provides tailored intelligence based on expeditionary profiles in littoral areas.

Non-Military Organizations

Central Intelligence Agency gathers, analyzes, and produces most of the nation's HUMINT. HUMINT may be able to provide targeteers with information not available though other intelligence collection methods. This may be particularly important in the case of terrorist organizations, which are often distributed networks with limited physical infrastructure. HUMINT is absolutely essential for analysis of such organizations.

Department of State, Bureau of Intelligence and Research (INR). As the lead foreign affairs agency and the enabler of US diplomacy, the State Department has a unique perspective on the nations of the world. Such insight, as collected, analyzed, and produced by INR, can be extremely influential when planning, executing, and assessing military operations. Intelligence concerning political and military leaders, cultural trends and thoughts, and economics—to name just a few areas—can give Airmen intelligence that ties military strategy to the entire spectrum of national power, which can be essential for a truly effects-based approach to conflict. Even from a purely military standpoint, such intelligence can enhance understanding of adversary motivations, helping to influence or bend them to our will...the ultimate goal in any operation.

Department of Homeland Security (DHS). Encompassing Citizen and Immigration Services, Customs and Border Patrol, Transportation Security, the Secret Service, and the Coast Guard, DHS, with its three primary missions—prevent terrorist attacks within the United States, reduce America's vulnerability to terrorism, and minimize the damage from potential attacks and natural disasters—has a wealth of intelligence on enemies, and potential enemies, of the US. Although DHS looks "inward," air and space planners may be able to "connect the dots" and utilize DHS-derived intelligence when it leads to foreign-based terrorist organizations and infrastructures.

Department of Justice (DOJ). With subordinate organizations such as the Federal Bureau of Investigation and the Drug Enforcement Administration, DOJ-derived information, like that of the DHS, may help focus targeting efforts when it leads to foreign-based terrorist organizations and infrastructures.

GLOSSARY

Abbreviations and Acronyms

AAC	Air Armaments Center
ACC	Air Combat Command
ACFT	analysis, correlation, and fusion team
ACO	airspace coordination order
AETC	Air Education and Training Command
AFB	Air Force base
AFDD	Air Force doctrine document
AFIWC	Air Force Information Warfare Center
AFMIC	Air Force Medical Intelligence Center
AFNOSC	Air Force Network Operations and Security Center
AFOTTP	Air Force operational tactics, techniques, and procedures
AFTTP	Air Force tactics, techniques, and procedures
AIG	air intelligence group
AIS	air intelligence squadron
ALLOREQ	allocation request
AOC	air and space operations center
AOD	air and space operations directive
AOG	air and space operations group
ASOC	air support operations center
ATO	air tasking order
AWACS	Airborne Warning and Control System
AWPD-1	Air War Planning Document-1
BCD	battlefield coordination detachment
BDA	battle damage assessment
BE#	basic encyclopedia number
BE / UID	basic encyclopedia number and ten-digit unit identification numbers
BFT	blue force tracking
C2	command and control
C2W	command and control warfare
CA	campaign assessment
CAOC	combined air and space operations center
CAP	crisis action planning
CAS	close air support
CAWG	combined assessment working group
CD	collateral damage
CDM	collateral damage methodology
CEWG	combined effects working group
CENTAF	Central Air Forces
CFACC	combined force air and space component commander

CFC	combined force commander
CIA	Central Intelligence Agency
CIB	combined integration board
CID	combat identification
CJCSI	Chairman, Joint Chiefs of Staff instruction
CMSA	cruise missile support agency
COA	course of action
COD	combat operations division
COG	center of gravity
COMAFFOR	commander, Air Force forces
CONOPS	concept of operations
CONPLAN	contingency plan
CONUS	continental United States
CPD	combat plans division
CWF	combat weather flight
DCGS	distributed common ground/surface systems
DGS	distributed ground station
DHS	Department of Homeland Security
DIA	Defense Intelligence Agency
DISA	Defense Information Systems Agency
DOD	Department of Defense
DOJ	Department of Justice
DPI	desired point of impact
DTRA	Defense Threat Reduction Agency
EBO	effects-based operation
EDA	estimated damage assessment
EOB	enemy order of battle
F2T2EA	find, fix, track, target, engage, assess
FA	functional assessment
FISINT	foreign instrumentation signal intelligence
FRAGO	fragmentary order
FSCM	fire support coordination measure
GAT	guidance, apportionment, and targeting (now called TET)
GCC	Global Cryptologic Center
GEOINT	geospatial intelligence
GPS	global positioning system
HAE	height above ellipsoid
HUMINT	human intelligence
IADS	integrated air defense system

IMINT	imagery intelligence
INFLTREP	inflight report
INR	Department of State Intelligence and Research Division
INSCOM	Intelligence and Security Command
IO	information operations
IOT	information operations team
IPB	intelligence preparation of the battlespace
IQT	initial qualification training
ISR	intelligence, surveillance and reconnaissance
ISRD	intelligence, surveillance and reconnaissance division
IW	information warfare
J-2	intelligence directorate of a joint staff
J2T	joint force intelligence directorate deputy director for targets
J/CFACC	joint/combined force air and space component commander
JAC	joint analysis center
JAEP	joint air and space estimate process
JA	judge advocate
JAOC	joint air and space operations center
JAOP	joint air and space operations plan
JAWG	joint assessment working group
JCS	Joint Chiefs of Staff
JDAM	joint direct attack munition
JDPI	joint designated point of impact
JEWG	joint effects working group
JFACC	joint force air and space component commander
JFC	joint force commander
JFSOCC	joint force special operations component commander
JIB	joint integration board
JIOC	joint intelligence operations center
JIPCL	joint integrated prioritized collection list
JIPTL	joint integrated prioritized target list
JMEM	joint munitions effectiveness manual
JP	joint publication
JSpOC	joint space operations center
JTCB	joint targeting coordination board
JTCG/ME	Joint Technical Coordinating Committee for Munitions Effectiveness
JTF	joint task force
JTL	joint target list
JWAC	Joint Warfare Analysis Center
LOAC	law of armed conflict
LNO	liaison officer
MAAP	master air attack plan

MAJCOM	major command
MASINT	measurement and signature intelligence
MCIA	Marine Corps intelligence activity
MEA	munitions effects assessment
MISREP	mission report
MOE	measure of effect
MOP	measure of performance
MQT	mission qualification training
MSIC	Missile and Space Intelligence Center
MSL	mean sea level
NA	national assessment
NAF	numbered air force
NASIC	National Air and Space Intelligence Center
NGA	National Geospatial Intelligence Agency
NGIC	National Ground Intelligence Agency
NIST	national intelligence support team
NMIC	National Maritime Intelligence Center
NSA	National Security Agency
NSL	no-strike list
OA	operational assessment
OAT	operational assessment team
OE	operational environment
OEF	Operation ENDURING FREEDOM
OGA	other governmental agency
OIF	Operation IRAQI FREEDOM
ONI	Office of Naval Intelligence
OPLAN	operation plan
OSINT	opens-source intelligence
PACAF	Pacific Air Forces
PBA	predictive battlespace awareness
PDA	physical damage assessment
POL	petroleum, oil, and lubricants
POW	prisoner of war
ROE	rules of engagement
RTL	restricted target list
SA	situational awareness
SAM	surface-to-air-missile
SD	strategy division
SI	success indicator
SIDO	Senior Intelligence Duty Officer
SIGINT	signals intelligence

SOF	special operations forces
SOLE	special operations liaison element
SORTIEALOT	sortie allotment message
SOSA	system of system analysis
SPINS	special instructions
SROE	standing rules of engagement
TA	tactical assessment
TACP	tactical air control party
TBMCS	Theater Battle Management Core System
TET	targeting effects team (formerly called GAT)
TNL	target nomination list
TPFDD	time-phased force and deployment data
TSA	target systems analysis
TST	time sensitive targets
USAAC	United States Army Air Corps
USAFE	United States Air Forces Europe
USJFCOM	United States Joint Forces Command
USSOCOM	United States Special Operations Command
USSTRATCOM	United States Strategic Command
USTRANSCOM	United States Transportation Command
WMD	weapons of mass destruction

Definitions

action. Performance of an activity. Actions are taken to achieve intended effects. Actions can be kinetic (physical, material) or non-kinetic (logical, behavioral). Actions are invariably tactical, usually producing tactical-level direct effects; subsequent causal linkages will determine the nature of higher-order indirect effects. (AFDD 2-1.9)

air and space expeditionary task force. A deployed numbered Air Force (NAF) or command echelon immediately subordinate to a NAF provided as the US Air Force component command committed to a joint operation. Also called **AETF.** (JP 1-02) [*The organizational manifestation of Air Force forces afield. The AETF provides a joint force commander with a task-organized, integrated package with the appropriate balance of force, sustainment, control, and force protection.*] {Italicized words in brackets apply only to the Air Force and are offered for clarity.}

air and space power. The synergistic application of air, space, and information systems to project global strategic military power. (AFDD 1)

allocation. In a general sense, distribution of limited resources among competing requirements for employment. Specific allocations (e.g., air sorties, nuclear weapons, forces, and transportation) are described as allocation of air sorties, nuclear weapons, etc. See also **allocation (air)** (JP 1-02)

allocation (air): The translation of the air apportionment decision into total numbers of sorties by aircraft type available for each operation or task. See also **allocation.** (JP 1-02) [*The translation of the air apportionment decision into total numbers of sorties or missions by weapon system type available for each operation or task*] {Italicized words in brackets apply only to the Air Force and are offered for clarity.}

apportionment. In the general sense, distribution for planning of limited resources among competing requirements. Specific apportionments (e.g., air sorties and forces for planning). (JP 1-02)

apportionment (air). The determination and assignment of the total expected effort by percentage and/or by priority that should be devoted to the various air operations for a given period of time. Also called **air apportionment.** (JP 1-02)

assessment. 1. Analysis of the security, effectiveness, and potential of an existing or planned intelligence activity. (JP 1-02) [*The evaluation of progress toward the creation of effects and the achievement of objectives and end state conditions.*] {Italicized words in brackets apply only to the Air Force and are offered for clarity.}

battle rhythm. A commander's pace, pattern, or systematic process used to plan and execute an engagement, battle, or campaign. (AFDD 2-1.9)

blue force tracking. The employment of techniques to identify US, allied, and coalition forces for the purposes of providing commanders enhanced situational awareness and reducing fratricide. Also called **BFT.** (AFDD 2-1.9)

campaign. A series of related military operations aimed at accomplishing a strategic or operational objective within a given time and space. (JP 1–02)

campaign assessment. The joint force commander's broad qualitative and analytical determination of the overall campaign progress, effectiveness of operations and recommendations for future action. Also called **CA.** (AFDD 2)

campaign plan. A plan for a series of related military operations aimed at accomplishing a strategic or operational objective within a given time and space. (JP 1–02)

cascading effect. An indirect effect that ripples through an adversary system, usually affecting other systems. Typically, cascading effects flow throughout the levels of war and are the result of interdependencies or linkages among multiple adversary systems. (AFDD 2-1.2)

causal linkage. An explanation of why an action or effect will cause or contribute to a given effect (AFDD 2)

centers of gravity. Those characteristics, capabilities or sources of power from which a military force derives its freedom of action, physical strength or will to fight. Also called **COGs.** (JP 1-02) [*In Air Force terms, a COG is a primary source of moral (i.e., political leadership, social dynamics, cultural values, or religion) or physical (i.e., military, industrial, or economic) strength from which a nation, alliance, or military force in a given strategic, operational, or tactical context derives its freedom of action, physical strength, or will to fight*] {Italicized words in brackets apply only to the Air Force and are offered for clarity.}

collateral damage. Unintentional or incidental injury or damage to persons or objects that would not be lawful military targets in the circumstances ruling at the time. Such damage is not unlawful so long as it is not excessive in light of the overall military advantage anticipated from the attack. (JP 1-02)

combat identification. The capability to attain an accurate characterization of detected objects in the joint battlespace to the extent that high confidence, timely application of military options and weapons resources can occur. Depending on the situation and the operational decisions that must be made, this characterization may be limited to "enemy," "friend," or "neutral." In other situations, other characterizations may be required—including, but not limited to class, type, nationality, mission configuration, status, and intent. Also call **CID.** (AFDD 2-1.9)

combined force commander. A general term applied to a combatant commander, subunified commander, or combined task force commander authorized to exercise combatant command (command authority) or operational control over a joint force. Also called **CFC.** (JP 1–02)

command and control. The exercise of authority and direction by a properly designated commander over assigned and attached forces in the accomplishment of the mission. Command and control functions are performed through an arrangement of personnel, equipment, communications, facilities, and procedures employed by a commander in planning, directing, coordinating, and controlling forces and operations in the accomplishment of the mission. Also called **C2.** (JP 0-2)

cumulative effect. An effect resulting from the aggregation of multiple, contributory direct or indirect effects. (AFDD 2-1.9)

deliberate targeting. The part of the tasking process for prosecuting targets that are detected, identified, and developed in sufficient time to schedule actions against them in tasking cycle products such as the air tasking order. (AFDD 2-1.9)

direct effect. First-order result of an action with no intervening effect between action and outcome. Usually immediate, physical, and readily recognizable (e.g., weapons employment results). (AFDD 2-1.9)

dynamic targeting. The part of the tasking process for prosecuting targets that are not detected, identified, or developed in time to be included in deliberate targeting, and therefore have not had actions scheduled against them. (AFDD 2-1.9)

effect indicator. Independent, qualitative or quantitative condition(s) that indicates the achievement of an effect. (AFDD 2-1.9)

effect. 1. The physical or behavioral state of a system that results from an action, a set of actions, or another effect. 2. The result, outcome, or consequence of an action. 3. A change to a condition, behavior, or degree of freedom (AFDD 2-1.9)

effects-based operations. Operations that are planned, executed, assessed, and adapted to influence or change systems or capabilities in order to achieve desired outcomes. Also called **EBO**. (AFDD 2)

emerging target. A potential target, which, upon initial detection, meets sufficient criteria to be considered and further developed. The criticality and time sensitivity of the potential target is initially undetermined. (AFDD 2-1.9)

end state. The set of conditions that needs to be achieved to resolve the situation or conflict on satisfactory terms, as defined by appropriate authority. (AFDD 2).

geospatial information and services. The concept for collection, information extraction, storage, dissemination, and exploitation of geodetic, geomagnetic, imagery (both commercial and national source), gravimetric, aeronautical, topographic, hydrographic, littoral, cultural, and toponymic data accurately referenced to a precise location on the earth's surface. These data are used for military planning, training, and operations including navigation, mission planning, mission rehearsal, modeling, simulation and precise targeting. Geospatial information provides the basic framework for battlespace visualization. It is information produced by multiple sources to common interoperable data standards. It may be presented in the form of printed maps, charts, and publications; in digital simulation and modeling databases; in photographic form; or in the form of digitized maps and charts or attributed centerline data. Geospatial services include tools that enable users to access and manipulate data, and also includes instruction, training, laboratory support, and guidance for the use of geospatial data. (JP 1-02)

geospatial intelligence. The exploitation and analysis of imagery and geospatial information to describe, assess and visually depict physical features and geographically referenced activities on the earth. Also known as **GEOINT**. (AFDD 2-1.9)

indirect effect. A second, third, or nth-order effect created through an intermediate effect or causal linkage following a causal action. May be physical, psychological, functional, or systemic in nature. May be created in a cumulative, cascading, sequential, or parallel manner. An indirect effect is often delayed and typically is more difficult to recognize and assess than a direct effect. (AFDD 2-1.9)

intended effect. A proactively sought effect. (AFDD 2-1.9)

information operations. The integrated employment of the core capabilities of electronic warfare, computer network operations, psychological operations, military deception, and operations security, in concert with specified supporting and related capabilities, to influence, disrupt, corrupt or usurp adversarial human and automated decision making while protecting our own. Also called **IO**. (JP 3-13. This term and its definition approved for inclusion in the next edition of JP 1-02.)

intelligence preparation of the battlespace. An analytical methodology employed to reduce uncertainties concerning the enemy, environment, and terrain for all types of operations. Intelligence preparation of the battlespace builds an extensive database for each potential area in which a unit may be required to operate. The database is then analyzed in detail to determine the impact of the enemy, environment, and terrain on operations and presents it in graphic form. Intelligence preparation of the battlespace is a continuing process. Also called **IPB**. (JP 1-02)

joint. Connotes activities, operations, organizations, etc., in which elements of two or more Military Departments participate. (JP 1–02)

joint target list. A consolidated list of selected targets considered to have military significance in the combatant commander's area of responsibility. Also called **JTL**. (JP 1-02)

joint integrated prioritized target list. A prioritized list of targets and associated data approved by the joint force commander or designated representative and maintained by a joint force. Targets and priorities are derived from the recommendations of components in conjunction with their proposed operations supporting the joint force commander's objectives and guidance. Also called **JIPTL**. (JP 1-02)

kinetic. Relating to actions that involve the forces and energy of moving bodies, including physical damage to or destruction of targets through use of bombs, missiles, bullets, and similar projectiles. (AFDD 2-1.9)

law of armed conflict. See **law of war.** Also called **LOAC**. (JP 1-02)

law of war. That part of international law that regulates the conduct of armed hostilities. Also called **the law of armed conflict.** (JP 1-02)

link. A behavioral, physical, or functional relationship between nodes in a system. (AFDD 2-1.9)

maneuver. 1. A movement to place ships, aircraft, or land forces in a position of advantage over the enemy. 2. A tactical exercise carried out at sea, in the air, on the ground, or on a map in imitation of war. 3. The operation of a ship, aircraft, or vehicle to cause it to perform desired movements. 4. Employment of forces in the battlespace through movement in combination with fires to achieve a position of advantage in respect to the enemy in order to accomplish the mission. (JP 1-02) [*Air and space power is a maneuver element in its own right, co-equal with land and maritime power; as such, it is no longer merely a supporting force to surface combat. As a maneuver element, it can be supported by surface forces in attaining its assigned objectives.*] {Italicized words in brackets apply only to the Air Force and are offered for clarity.}

measures and indicators. Encompassing term for the various criteria used to evaluate progress within the assessment process (AFDD 2-1.9)

measure of effect. Independent qualitative or quantitative empirical measure assigned to an intended effect, against which the effect's achievement is assessed. Also call **MOE**. (AFDD 2-1.9)

measure of performance. A quantitative empirical measure of achieved actions against associated planned/required actions and against which a task's or other action's accomplishment, is assessed. Also called **MOP**. (AFDD 2-1.9)

national assessment. A broad, overarching review of the effectiveness of national security strategy and whether national leadership's objectives for a particular operation or campaign are being met. Also called **NA**. (AFDD 2-1.9)

node. A tangible entity that is a physical, functional, or behavioral element of a system. (AFDD 2-1.9)

non-kinetic. Relating to actions that produce effects without direct use of the force or energy of moving objects, including such means as electromagnetic radiation, directed energy, information operations, etc. (AFDD 2-1.9)

no-strike list. A list of geographic areas, complexes, or installations not planned for capture or destruction. Attacking these may violate the law of armed conflict or interfere with friendly relations with indigenous personnel or governments. Also called **NSL**. (JP 1-02) [*The no-strike list is a list of geographic areas, complexes, installations, or personnel not planned for capture or destruction. Attacking personnel may violate LOAC or interfere with friendly relations with indigenous personnel or governments.*] {Italicized words in brackets apply only to the Air Force and are offered for clarity.}

objective. 1. The clearly defined, decisive, and attainable goals towards which every military operation should be directed. 2. The specific target of the action taken (for example, a definite terrain feature, the seizure or holding of which is essential to the commander's plan, or, an enemy force or capability without regard to terrain features). See also **target**. (JP 1-02)

operational art. The employment of military forces to attain strategic and/or operational objectives through the design, organization, integration, and conduct of strategies, campaigns, major operations, and battles. Operational art translates the joint force commander's strategy into operational design and, ultimately, tactical action, by integrating the key activities at all levels of war. (JP 1-02)

operational assessment. A joint force components' evaluation of their achievement of their objectives, both tactical and operational, through assessment of effects, operational execution, environmental influences, and attainment of the objectives success indicators, in order to develop strategy recommendations. Also called OA. (AFDD 2-1.9)

operational control. Command authority that may be exercised by commanders at any echelon at or below the level of combatant command. Operational control is inherent in combatant command (command authority) and may be delegated within the command. When forces are transferred between combatant commands, the command relationship the gaining commander will exercise (and the losing commander will relinquish) over these forces must be specified by the Secretary of Defense. Operational control is the authority to perform those functions of command over subordinate forces involving organizing and employing commands and forces, assigning tasks, designating objectives, and giving authoritative direction necessary to accomplish the mission. Operational control includes authoritative direction over all aspects of military operations and joint training necessary to accomplish missions assigned to the command. Operational control should be exercised through the commanders of subordinate organizations. Normally this authority is exercised through subordinate joint force commanders and Service and/or functional component commanders. Operational control normally provides full authority to organize commands and forces and to employ those forces as the commander in operational control considers necessary to accomplish assigned missions; it does not, in and of itself, include authoritative direction for logistics or matters of administration, discipline, internal organization, or unit training. Also called OPCON. (JP1-02)

operational level of war. The level of war at which campaigns and major operations are planned, conducted, and sustained to accomplish strategic objectives within theaters or other operational areas. Activities at this level link tactics and strategy by establishing operational objectives needed to accomplish the strategic objectives, sequencing events to achieve the operational objectives, initiating actions, and applying resources to bring about and sustain these events. These activities imply a broader dimension of time or space than do tactics; they ensure the logistic and administrative support of tactical forces, and provide the means by which tactical successes are exploited to achieve strategic objectives. (JP 1-02)

predictive battlespace awareness. The situational awareness needed to develop patterns of behavior, constraints, and opportunities of geography, topography, culture, environment, and forces that allow us to misdirect, predict, and pre-empt our adversaries. Also called PBA. (AFDD 2-1.9)

psychological operations. Planned operations to convey selected information and indicators to foreign audiences to influence their emotions, motives, objective reasoning, and ultimately the behavior of foreign governments, organizations, groups, and individuals. The purpose of psychological operations is to induce or reinforce foreign attitudes and behavior favorable to the originator's objectives. Also called **PSYOP**. (JP 1–02)

reachback. The process of obtaining products, services, and applications, or forces, or equipment, or material from organizations that are not forward deployed. (JP 1-02)

restricted target list. A list of restricted targets nominated by elements of the joint force and approved by the joint force commander. This list also includes restricted targets directed by higher authorities. Also called **RTL.** (JP 1-02) [*A list of targets that have specific restrictions imposed upon them. Actions that exceed specific restrictions are prohibited until coordinated and approved by the establishing headquarters. Targets are restricted because certain types of actions against them may have negative political, cultural, law of armed conflict or propaganda implications, or may interfere with projected friendly operations. The RTL is nominated by elements of the joint force and approved by the combined force commander. This list also includes restricted targets directed by higher authorities.*] {Words in brackets apply only to the Air Force and are offered for clarity.}

rules of engagement. Directives issued by competent military authority that delineate the circumstances and limitations under which United States forces will initiate and/or continue combat engagement with other forces encountered. Also called **ROE.** (JP 1-02)

strategic attack. Offensive action conducted by command authorities action aimed at generating effects that most directly achieve our national security objectives by affecting an adversary's leadership, conflict-sustaining resources, and/or strategy. (AFDD 2-1.2)

strategic level of war. The level of war at which a nation, often as a member of a group of nations, determines national or multinational (alliance or coalition) security objectives and guidance, and develops and uses national resources to accomplish these objectives. Activities at this level establish national and multinational military objectives; sequence initiatives; define limits and assess risks for the use of military and other instruments of national power; develop global plans or theater war plans to achieve these objectives; and provide military forces and other capabilities in accordance with strategic plans. (JP 1–02)

success indicator. The conditions indicating the progress toward and/or achievement of an objective or end-state condition. Also called **SI.** (AFDD 2-1.9)

tactical assessment. The overall determination of the effectiveness of tactical operations. This consists of several elements: physical damage assessment, functional assessment, munitions effectiveness assessment, estimated damage analysis, lower-intensity conflict assessment, weather effects, and logistic status. Formerly known (in less comprehensive form) as combat assessment or CA. Also called **TA** (AFDD 2-1.9)

tactical control. Command authority over assigned or attached forces or commands, or military capability or forces made available for tasking, that is limited to the detailed direction and control of movements or maneuvers within the operational area necessary to accomplish missions or tasks assigned. Tactical control is inherent in operational control. Tactical control may be delegated to, and exercised at any level at or below the level of combatant command. When forces are transferred between combatant commands, the command relationship the gaining commander will exercise (and the losing commander will relinquish) over these forces must be specified by the Secretary of Defense. Tactical control provides sufficient authority for controlling and directing the application of force or tactical use of combat support assets within the assigned mission or task. Also called **TACON**. (JP 1–02)

tactical level of war. The level of war at which battles and engagements are planned and executed to accomplish military objectives assigned to tactical units or task forces. Activities at this level focus on the ordered arrangement and maneuver of combat elements in relation to each other and to the enemy to achieve combat objectives. (JP 1–02)

target. 1. An area, complex, installation, force, equipment, capability, function, individual, group, system, or behavior identified for possible action to support the commander's objectives, guidance, and intent. Targets fall into two general categories: deliberate and dynamic. 2. In intelligence usage, a country, area, installation, agency, or person against which intelligence operations are directed. 3. An area designated and numbered for future firing. 4. In gunfire support usage, an impact burst that hits the target. Also called **TGT.** (JP 1-02)

targeteer. Multi-disciplinary specialists highly trained in analyzing targets and developing targeting solutions to support the commander's objectives. (AFDD 2-1.9)

targeting. The process of selecting and prioritizing targets and matching the appropriate response to them, taking account of operational requirements and capabilities. (JP 1-02). [*The part of the tasking process for selecting and prioritizing targets and matching appropriate actions to those targets to create specific desired effects that achieve objectives, taking account of operational requirements and capabilities.*] {Italicized words in brackets apply only to the Air Force and are offered for clarity.}

time-sensitive targets. Those targets requiring immediate response because they pose (or will soon pose) a danger to friendly forces or are highly lucrative, fleeting targets of opportunity. Also called **TSTs.** (JP 1-02)

weaponeering. The process of determining the quantity of a specific type of lethal or nonlethal weapons required to achieve a specific level of damage to a given target, considering target vulnerability, weapons effect, munitions delivery accuracy, damage criteria, probability of kill, and weapon reliability. (JP 1-02) [*Weaponeering is the part of the tasking process for estimating the quantity and types of lethal and non-lethal weapons needed to achieve desired effects against specific targets.*] {Italicized words in brackets apply only to the Air Force and are offered for clarity.}